The Bertrand Bottles

The Bertrand Bottles

*A Study of 19th-Century Glass
And Ceramic Containers*

by Ronald R. Switzer

NATIONAL PARK SERVICE
U.S. DEPARTMENT OF THE INTERIOR

WASHINGTON 1974

As the Nation's principal conservation agency, the Department of the Interior has basic responsibilities for water, fish, wildlife, mineral, land, park, and recreational resources. Indian and Territorial affairs are other major concerns of America's "Department of Natural Resources." The Department works to assure the wisest choice in managing all our resources so each will make its full contribution to a better United States—now and in the future.

This publication is the result of a study of an archeological and historic site on Federal land for which the National Park Service has had responsibilities. It is printed at the Government Printing Office, and may be purchased from the Superintendent of Documents, Washington, D.C. 20402. Price $2.15 (paper cover). Stock Number 024–005–00529–3

Library of Congress Cataloging in Publication Data

Switzer, Ronald R
    The Bertrand bottles.

    (Publications in archeology, no. 12)
    Bibliography: p.
    Supt. of Docs. no.: I 29.59: 12.
    1. Bottles—United States. 2. Bertrand (Steamboat)
I. Title. II. Series.
E51.U75 no. 12   [NK5440.B6]   666'.19   72-600353

Publications in Archeology *

Archeological Research Series

1. Archeology of the Bynum Mounds, Mississippi (PB 177 061).**
2. Archeological Excavations in Mesa Verde National Park, Colorado, 1950 (PB 177 062).**
3. Archeology of the Funeral Mound, Ocmulgee National Monument, Georgia (PB 177 063).**
4. Archeological Excavations at Jamestown, Virginia (PB 177 064).**
5. The Hubbard Site and other Tri-wall Structures in New Mexico and Colorado.
6. Search for the Cittie of Ralegh, Archeological Excavations at Fort Raleigh National Historic Site, North Carolina.
7A. The Archeological Survey of Wetherill Mesa, Mesa Verde National Park, Colorado (Wetherill Mesa Studies).
7B. Environment of Mesa Verde, Colorado (Wetherill Mesa Studies).
7C. Big Juniper House, Mesa Verde National Park, Colorado (Wetherill Mesa Studies).
7D. Mug House, Mesa Verde National Park, Colorado (Wetherill Mesa Studies).
8. Excavations in the 17th-Century Jumano Pueblo, Gran Quivira, New Mexico.
9. Excavations at Tse-ta'a, Canyon de Chelly National Monument, Arizona

Publications in Archeology

10. Ruins Stabilization in the Southwestern United States
11. The Steamboat Bertrand: History, Excavation and Architecture
12. The Bertrand Bottles: A Study of 19th-Century Glass and Ceramic Containers

Anthropological Papers

1. An Introduction to Middle Missouri Archeology
2. Like-a-Fishhook Village and Fort Berthold, Garrison Reservoir, North Dakota

*Concurrent with the establishment of the Office of Professional Publications, National Park Service, the name *Archeological Research Series* has been changed to *Publications in Archeology.* The numbering of the volumes will not change. The series entitled *Anthropological Papers* is discontinued.

**These publications are no longer available from the Superintendent of Documents. They may be ordered by title (and parenthetical code number) by writing to: Clearinghouse, U.S. Department of Commerce, Springfield, Virginia 22151. These reports are available in two forms: microfiche at 95 cents per document, or paper copy at $6.00 per volume, prepaid.

Preface

The purpose of this study is to bring together temporal and functional information for more than 6,000 bottles recovered from the steamer *Bertrand* in 1968-1969. Presumably, commercial bottles like those described were common during the Civil War era, but now have become relatively rare. They are of special significance because their study brings into focus the economic and technological conditions of the 1860's, and provides an important means of dating other historic sites. Their destination was the mining districts of Montana Territory, where their contents were intended to satisfy the desires of miners, sod busters, wranglers and travelers.

Although there are many books available on the subject of bottles, most are simply descriptive texts that contain little information relating to classification, function, or history. The need for inclusion of all three subjects in a bottle text is very great indeed, if for no other reason than to bring order to a menagerie of objects, and to insure that bottle specialists and historians all speak the same language. This work provides a classification and description of physical attributes of bottles from the *Bertrand*. Where known, information about bottle manufacturers, details of fabrication, and business histories of product manufacturers, wholesalers, and consignees has been included. Perhaps equally important are descriptions of shipping crates and the manner in which the bottles were packed. Hundreds of whole specimens taken from the *Bertrand* were found in their original crates. The latter often exhibited the stenciled names and addresses of wholesalers and manufacturers. In addition, newspapers, almanacs and broadsides which composed part of the packing material in some crates were of great value in documenting the bottles and their contents. Finally, many bottles still retain their corks, seals and paper labels, and should not be discounted for what they contribute to the documentation of this period collection.

Details of bottle fabrication and the identification of bottle producers are not necessarily beyond the scope of this volume, although such information in most cases is meager. To delete these details would be to withhold something of worth to future researchers. Even though some specimens bear embossed designs, letters and marks, it is unfortunate that most of their makers are still unknown. These marks, which presumably were peculiar to specific companies, are included in the hope that they will be of use to others in accurately determining the identity of bottle factories, when they operated, and in what years particular marks appeared on their products.

In short, this study is meant to be a reference for archeologists, historians, curators and others who are charged with the task of classifying, describing, and interpreting bottles in collections of nineteenth century glass.

This work could not have been undertaken without the cooperative support of the National Park Service and the Bureau of Sport Fisheries and Wildlife. I especially wish to acknowledge Rex L. Wilson, Acting Chief, Division of Archeology and Anthropology, Office of Archeology and Historic Preservation, upon whose bottle classification system I have so heavily relied. I am indebted to Wilfred D. Logan, Chief, Midwest Archeological Center, and to Jackson W. Moore, Staff Archeologist, for their helpful criticism. Special thanks go to Wayne Nelson, Staff Photographer, Midwest Archeological Center, and Jerry Livingston, Technical Illustrator, Midwest Archeological Center, for their assistance in preparing illustrations. Finally, on the staff of the Bertrand Conservation Laboratory, I am grateful for the help of Valerie Reiley, Secretary, Maia Sornson, Park Technician, and most capable Curator, Mary Dorinda Partsch.

R.R.S.

September, 1972

Contents

Illustrations

Introduction

Once in a very great while a few historic artifacts are found which contribute significantly to our knowledge of a particular period. Rarer still is the find of a 19th-century steamboat containing a cargo composed of thousands of pounds of artifacts of infinite variety. However, the relative rarity of these artifacts is overshadowed to a considerable degree by what can be translated from their analysis about the economy, technology, and life of contemporaries who lost them in an unpredictable wreck more than 100 years ago.

The discovery of the steamer *Bertrand* in 1968 marked the end of nearly a century of periodic searching for the vessel. The *Bertrand* was built in Wheeling, West Virginia, in the summer of 1864 (Petsche, 1970, p. 3), and subsequently was purchased by the Montana and Idaho Transportation Line of St. Louis, Mo. The low draft steamer was 161 feet long, and had a 32-foot, 9-inch beam. Commanded by James A. Yore, she left her berth in St. Louis for Fort Benton in Montana Territory on March 18, 1865, bearing at least ten passengers and a cargo estimated to have weighed well in excess of 251 tons (*ibid.*,p.4). On April 1, 1865, the boat struck a snag and sank in the Missouri River at Portage La Force near De Soto Landing in Nebraska Territory. No lives were lost but the insurer's salvage boat was unable, after two attempts, to recover the major part of the

cargo of agricultural and mining supplies, household paraphernalia (Switzer, 1972, pp. 5-7; 1971, pp. 6-10), clothing (D'Amato, 1971; Schweiger, 1971; Switzer, 1972, pp. 417-426), canned and bottled foodstuffs, bitters, wines and munitions (Switzer, 1971, pp. 5-6). Nevertheless, these contemporary salvors appear to have enlarged the bow hatch and to have recovered all but 684 pounds of the mercury the boat carried. It has been estimated that the *Bertrand* may have carried as much as 35,000 pounds of the metal in wrought iron carboys.

In 1968 and 1969, the remainder of this voluminous collection was removed from the *Bertrand* by its discoverers, Sam Corbino and Jesse Pursell. They were assisted and supervised in this effort by archeologists of the National Park Service and personnel of the Bureau of Sport Fisheries and Wildlife. The artifacts are presently housed in the Bertrand Conservation Laboratory, at DeSoto National Wildlife Refuge near Missouri Valley, Iowa, where they are being cleaned, preserved, and catalogued by National Park Service specialists.

In relating the history of the *Bertrand*, it seems worthwhile to say something of the nature of steamboating on the Missouri River and to note some of the economic and technological developments at the end of the Civil War. Navigation of the Missouri by steam-

1

boat prior to the beginning of the 19th century was considered out of the question. Simple boats began using the Missouri as an avenue of trade about this time, and by 1805 a keelboat was taken to the head of navigation at Fort Benton by the famous Lewis and Clark Expedition (Chittenden, 1962, pp. 90-91). Other keelboats soon followed, some bearing as much as 15 tons of foodstuffs, hardware and trade goods. Almost overnight this avenue of commerce became a two-way shipping lane.

The continued growth of commercial navigation on the Missouri rose in response to at least three demands of the times. The first of these was directly related to developing a means of transporting furs from the Rocky Mountains to eastern markets during the first half of the 19th century (*ibid.*, pp.133-134). The second demand was for an efficient means of transporting men and supplies to the upper reaches of the Missouri to establish military posts and secure ownership of the territory for the United States after 1804. Finally, during the 1860's, when the fur trade began to decline and gold was discovered in Idaho and Montana, a substantial demand developed for tools and supplies in the mining districts. As time passed, larger boats tried to ascend the river, and, with the advent of steam engines and the development of the shallow draft steamboat in the first decade of the 19th century, steady advances were made upstream. In 1819 the *Western Engineer*, a government boat of the ill-fated Yellowstone Expedition, ascended the river as far as Council Bluffs. Forty years later, the *Chippewa*, owned by the American Fur Company, reached the head of navigation on the Missouri near Fort Benton in Montana Territory, and became a forerunner of river trade which was to continue for nearly a century (*ibid.*, p. 219).

The swift current, changing channel, eddies, snags and sand bars were major obstacles to commercial shipping, and the river took an unmerciful toll of steamboats. Captain H.M. Chittenden (1970, pp. 17-23) of the Missouri River Commission wrote in 1897 that in the preceeding 44 years 273 boats had been lost to the river, 193 of them wrecked on snags. With such a relentless toll, shipping companies doubled and tripled their charges for freight, but their losses never seemed to be covered. The *Bertrand*, which sank when she

struck a snag on her maiden voyage to the mountains, was valued at between $50,000 and $65,000 and her cargo at $100,000 to $300,000. Such losses were no small matter, even to prominent businessmen like two of her owners, John J. Roe and John G. Copelin, whose company's fleet included the steamer *Benton*, the *Yellowstone*, the *Fanny Ogden* and the *Deer Lodge* (Petsche, 1974; 1970, p. 4).

Despite the frailties of steamboats and losses to the river, commerce continued to grow, seldom waning even during the Civil War. The larger cities on the Missouri, particularly St. Louis, which owed its initial growth to the fur trade and the development of the lead industry, later owed their prosperity to the goods supplied to the mining districts in Idaho and Montana. Gold was discovered in southeastern Idaho, in 1860 and again two years later in southwestern Montana, fostering the growth of Bannock City and the beginning of Montana's mining boom (Lavender, 1965, pp. 319-320).

The territory of Montana was already becoming overcrowded when, in the fall of 1864, a second strike was made in Last Chance Gulch which ultimately produced 20 million dollars in gold, and caused a rush in the tide of humanity unlike any the West had ever seen. With the discovery came an increasing demand for tools, hardware, foodstuffs, and a few alcoholic luxuries that overland transport simply could not provide in adequate volume. During the navigable months of the middle 1860's, steamboats landed cargo almost daily at Fort Benton. From there it was hauled overland in wagons to the mining camps where it brought phenomenal prices. Unfortunately, the steamers could only operate on a seasonal basis; none, it seemed, could fill the demands.

For the readers of this book, history has provided a more than adequate explanation for the volume and variety of bottled goods present in the cargo of the steamship *Bertrand*. She carried pickles, preserves, sauces, syrups, condiments, wines, liquors, and medicines which were impossible to produce on the American frontier, and which were difficult, if not at times impossible, to obtain without the aid of the river shipping industry.

There have been so many different kinds of bottles made in the United States in the past 200 years that historians and antiquarians must constantly exchange information if they are properly to identify, date, and classify them into an organized body of knowledge. Perhaps by describing what possibly is the largest collection of bottles ever recovered from a single historic period archeological site, an important chapter can be written about the glass making industry in America. More numerous and less aesthetic than decorative glass items, bottles often provide better information about the history of our country and some of its commercial products.

This is not meant to be a book for collectors, but rather a compendium of temporal and functional information concerning a single collection of commercial bottles of the Civil War era. Morphology has been classified, and the makers of the bottles were researched insofar as it was possible in hopes of assisting historians, curators, glass specialists, and interpreters. The size, color, shape, and method of manufacture of bottles are all of popular interest, but these must be recorded in a logical and systematic manner if they are to be useful in telling the complete story of American commercial glass. I have tried to make this more than a descriptive text by including material on bottle technology as well as information relating to the business histories of the companies which used the containers. All of this is history, but hopefully not history for its own sake. All too often as specialists we do not see the forest for getting locked in on the proverbial tree. It is a simple thing to describe a bottle (or bottles) in great detail, but quite another to say something significant about its manufacture, contents, or use. If the task has been fully accomplished in this book, so much the better; if it has not, the deficiency lies in the absence of companion information. So much more is needed in the way of historical information before we have a clear picture of the glass making and bottle fabricating industry in America. That the steamer *Bertrand* contained so complete a cargo when it sank was an historical accident, but one from which information will be taken for years to come.

I

Production Technology Of 19th-Century Bottles

It is hard to imagine a world without glass even though some of it, like ornamental pieces and tableware with their beauty of form, are relatively functionless compared to bottles, optics, and light bulbs. Scientists have long debated the properties of this miraculous substance (Brill, 1962, pp. 127-138) and its place of origin, but none doubt its antiquity. Most recognize that the tools and technology of its production and manufacture have changed very little in several thousand years.

It is common knowledge that all of the major techniques used to produce glass bottles and tableware were in existence by the beginning of the 19th century. The most important developments in American glass during this period were improvements and innovations in glass working and production. Between 1815 and the end of the Civil War, more than a dozen new or improved patents for glass furnaces were obtained in the United States alone. It was at this time that the "glory hole," a very small furnace for reheating a finished article to obliterate tool marks, came into use (McKearin and McKearin, 1971, p. 15). Other innovations included leers or annealing ovens and chambers, and the introduction of metal holding tongs with semicircular wooden jaws which did not mark molten glass during handling (*ibid.*, pp. 15, 18).

The most common method of producing bottles early in the 19th century was by blowing, and the shapes of hand blown bottles were determined by the tools, desires, and skills of the blower. The use of molds was less common. Hand blown or free-blown bottles of this period are usually lopsided and asymmetrical, and have smooth shiny surfaces devoid of designs and letters. Most of these bottles exhibit pontil scars or rough spots at the centers of their bases. These scars resulted from the attachment of pontils or holding rods to the bases with bits of molten glass. By these means, bottles could be held while the gaffers struck off their blowpipes and finished the lips of the apertures. Pontil scars, resulting from striking the pontil rods from the bases, were sometimes removed or smoothed over by fire polishing or grinding. The other steps required to produce free-blown glass objects are found in *American Glass* (McKearin and McKearin, 1971), and will not be described.

Another method for producing bottles was to form them in molds. Early in the 19th century, mold-blown or blown-in-mold bottles were made in two kinds of molds, full size contact molds and dip molds of various sizes, some containing patterns. A dip mold was composed of one piece, open at the top. When a pattern dip mold was employed, a gather of molten glass (called metal) was inserted in the mold and blown to impress the pattern in it. The pattern-impressed glass was then re-

5

moved from the mold and blown to the desired size. Patterns imparted by these molds are diffuse, with smooth or rounded edges, but mold marks are absent. The inner surface of pattern-molded-and-expanded ware bears a positive image of the pattern on the exterior. According to Lorrain (1968, p. 37), bottles and tableware produced by this method were common early in the century, but had practically disappeared by 1850.

Bottles blown in full contact molds may or may not exhibit mold marks or lines which resulted from molten glass seeping into hinge seams where the mold sections joined. Sometimes called blown-in-mold wares, the inner surfaces of bottles produced by this technique exhibit negative images of the raised patterns on their exteriors. Hinged molds, although known previously, were not widespread in this country until after 1810 when the three-piece mold made its appearance (McKearin and McKearin, 1971, pp. 427-428; Lorrain, 1968, p.38). The three-piece hinged mold consisted of a body mold and a two-piece mold for the shoulder and neck; the lip was hand finished.

About 1840, the two-piece hinged mold was introduced to the bottle making trade. The first of these were probably made of brass, but in five years iron molds were put into service. In the 10 years following 1840, two-piece iron molds began to replace their three-piece predecessors. Perhaps the most significant features of bottles produced in two-piece molds are the vertical mold lines which run the entire length of the bottles from the bases to the necks (Lorrain, 1968, pp. 39-40). Occasionally, these marks were removed by rotating the bottles in the molds while the glass was still molten. Mold lines disappeared on the upper necks because they were obliterated by reheating the glass to apply the lip finish. At about this same time, the lipping tool used for applying the finish to bottle apertures made its appearance, replacing the "laid on ring" of molten glass. The lipping tool consist-ed of a central plug which was inserted in the neck of the bottle, and two hinged patterned arms which clamped around the outside with a metal band. When the tool was rotated the arms formed the lip of the bottle and obliter-ated some of the mold marks (Lorrain, 1968, p. 40).

By 1857 the bottle making industry saw the invention of what may have been its most important tool, the snap case. This simple device completely replaced the pontil rod for holding bottles during the application of the lip finish. Composed of four curved arms which clamped around the bottle, it seldom left a mark on a finished piece, and it also eliminated sharp-edged pontil scars (*Encyclopedia Britannica*, 1949, vol. 10, p. 410).

After 1860, a large number of closures were invented in the United States, but most of them never achieved widespread popularity. Most of the bottles recovered from the steamer *Bertrand* were stoppered with corks, albeit some, such as those in champagne bottles, have clamps or bails to hold them in place. A few specimens contain glass stoppers with cork sleeves, and four chemical bottles have ground glass closures.

In 1861, the first lead glass medicine bottles appeared in America, and shortly thereafter tall, four-sided bottles with beveled corners and known as "French squares" were put on the market. It is suspected that the first lettered bottles, most of which were French squares or ornate types, made their appearance at about this time, and not after the Civil War as Moore (1924, pp. 255-256) and Lorraine (1968, p. 40) suggest, even though most molds were hand made until 1900. Hundreds of lettered bottles containing bitters were removed from the *Bertrand*, which places their date of manufacture at 1864, if not earlier. The presence of a number of small lead glass medicine bottles in the Bertrand collection bearing recessed lettered panels on two sides also tends to support this position.

II

Bottle Classification

The classification and documentation of bottles found in historic sites has become a matter of considerable urgency. With this in mind, the first problem was whether to devise a new classification system or search the literature for one that could be modified for use. Works by Lorrain (1968), the Ferraros (1966), Holscher (1965), Hunt (1959), Wilson (1961; 1961; 1974) and others have described some of the observable changes in the manufacture of bottles which were helpful in classifying and dating the Bertrand specimens. However, of the studies cited, Lorrain's (1968) article on 19th century glass and Wilson's (1961; 1974) studies of bottles on the military frontier were most helpful.

An existing bottle classification system was chosen, eliminating some duplication of effort. The system selected was devised by Rex L. Wilson (1961, pp. 2-6) of the National Park Service for use in ordering large collections of 19th-century bottles from Fort Union National Monument, New Mexico, and Fort Laramie National Historic Site, Wyoming. Using Wilson's system as a model, some of the descriptive categories have been modified, and several new ones have been added, but the salient features remain intact. Judging from the variety of shapes in use during the 19th century, it is probable that no classification system can be all-inclusive. The bottle classes, descriptive categories, and nomenclature used in the Bertrand Conservation Laboratory and in the text of this paper appear below and in figures 1 and 2 and table 1 to avoid confusion and disagreement resulting from their use:

Base: the lowermost part or bottom upon which a bottle stands or rests.

Body: the main part of a bottle, which is composed of one or more sides. The body of a bottle can generally be defined as that part of the wall or side usually perpendicular to the base, and which appears between the edge of the base and the point of change in vertical tangency of the side.

Kick-up: a steep rise or pushed-up part of the base. This feature is common in wine bottles.

Lip: the edge of the aperture.

Neck: the constricted part of a bottle which lies between the point of vertical tangency at the end or top of the shoulder and the lip of the orifice.

Neck finish: the addition of a collar or band of glass to the neck of a bottle at or near the lip of the orifice, or, the manipulation of the molten glass at the neck terminus of a bottle to produce a finished effect.

Orifice: mouth or aperture.

Shoulder: that part of a bottle which lies between the point of change in vertical tangency of the side and the base of the neck.

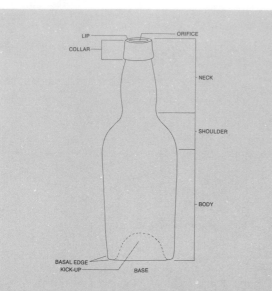

FIGURE 1. Key to bottle nomenclature.

FIGURE 2. Key to styles of neck finishes.

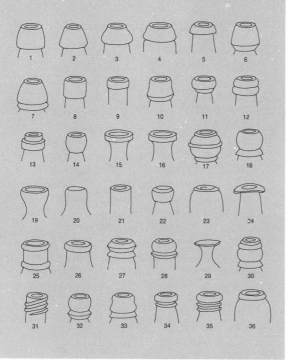

A major problem with any classification system involves the number of descriptive attributes that are desirable to distinguish types and subtypes. For the purpose of this study, when a group of bottles are similar morphologically but exhibit a variance in one major descriptive attribute or in several minor attributes, the largest number of bottles which are alike in all respects constitute a type. The remainder of the bottles, with variable attributes, are designated as subtypes. Groups of bottles which have or had identical or generically similar contents and/or closures, but which are different morphologically, are seperated into distinct types and subtypes.

All bottles from the *Bertrand* are free-blown or blown-in-mold varieties, and the latter exhibit the marks of two- or three-piece molds. Nearly all of the bottles have neck finishes showing the marks of lipping tools and the application of a separate piece of glass at or near the neck terminus.

The Bertrand bottles have been placed in six major groups or classes as follows: I, ale, beer, and stout; III, wine, whiskey, bitters, and other intoxicants; IV, toiletry bottles; V, culinary bottles; VI, ink containers; and VII, chemical and medicine bottles. (No bottles on the *Bertrand* were found to have contained soft drinks, i.e., Class II, a major grouping in Wilson's scheme.)

Detailed morphological information for all types and subtypes appear in the tables in the Appendix. Table 1 presents a key to characteristics of all types and subtypes enumerated in tables 2 through 13. Figure 2 provides an illustrative key to the styles of neck finishes.

CLASS I
ALE, BEER AND STOUT

The generic identity of the contents of most of the bottles in this class cannot be accurately determined. Twelve imported wheel-thrown stoneware bottles definitely contained ale, but the contents of 43 additional salt-glazed, wheel-thrown containers, and 21 amber glass bottles remain a mystery. Two of the latter are embossed to indicate that they may have contained ale, but the remainder are plain and closely resemble modern beer bottles in shape. However, inasmuch as the brewing industry did not begin to pasteurize beer until 1873, it is unlikely that the amber glass bottles contained the product. Unpasteurized beer had a very short shelf life and could not be exposed to alternating heat and cold, prolonged standing at room temperature, nor could it be shipped long distances (Arnold, 1933, p. 99). Ale, with its higher alcohol and undecomposed sugar content (*Webster*'s *New Twentieth Century Dictionary*,1964, pp. 44, 166) did not go stale or spoil quickly, and seems to have been a common beverage on the western frontier. No bottles recovered could definitely be identified as having contained beer or stout.

Class I, Type I, Subtypes 1a, 1b, 1c, 1d, 1e, 1f, 1g.

The collection of 43 ceramic ale containers have been divided into subtypes on the basis of variations in morphology (Table 2). All of the bottles are wheel-thrown, salt-glazed pottery, with little or no glaze on the bases. The lower bodies of the bottles are cream-colored, while the shoulders and necks are pale to dark yellow ochre.

Type 1 is composed of 24 whole bottles. The bases are flat to very slightly concave. The bodies of some bottles are stamped close to the base with the single letters: "J," "O," "W," "S," "L," "H," "D," "M," "C," or "B." The bottles are cylindrical and the shoulders curve gently inward in conical fashion. The necks terminate in double ring finishes. The upper

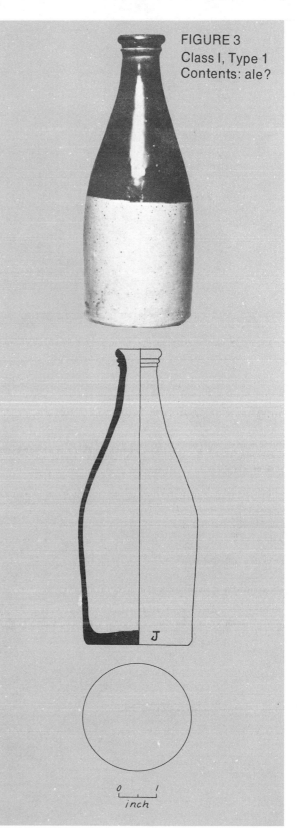

FIGURE 3
Class I, Type 1
Contents: ale?

J

0   1
inch

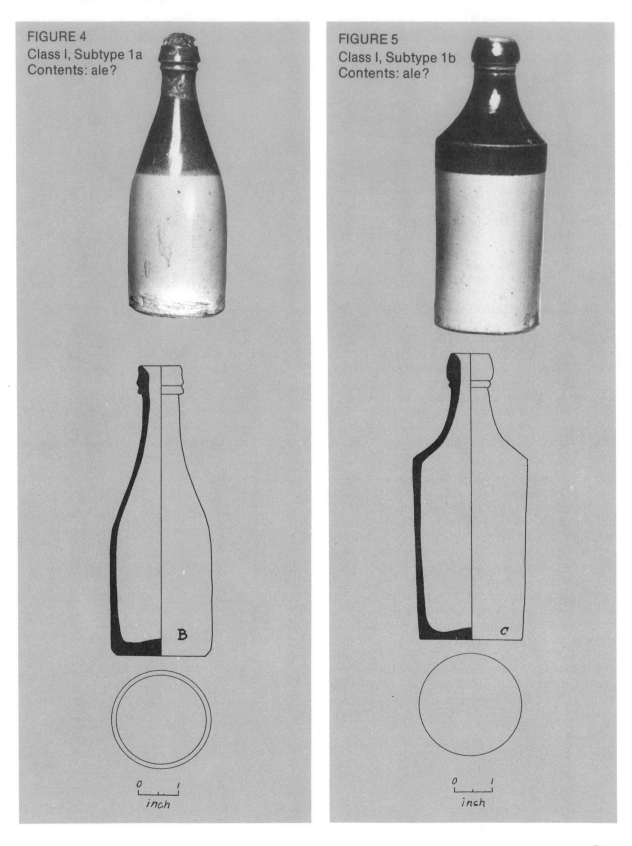

FIGURE 4
Class I, Subtype 1a
Contents: ale?

FIGURE 5
Class I, Subtype 1b
Contents: ale?

ring is larger than the lower, and exhibits a flat lip. The stoppers for the bottles are cork, held in place with thin wire bails. All of these specimens display remnants of thin foil about the apertures and on the necks (fig. 3). Dimensions: height, 8 inches; diameter of base, 2 15/16 inches; diameter of neck (outside), 1 3/16 inches (inside), 3/4 inch.

\The body of Subtype 1a is similar to that of Type 1. This bottle, the only one of its kind in the collection, was not as heavily glazed as the others, giving it a dull finish. The collar is slightly concave in profile, and has a sharp basal edge. The lip slants downward into the orifice. Beneath the collar is a narrow ring, also bearing a sharp edge. Approximately 1/4 inch up from the base, the letter "B" is stamped into the body. The bottle is sealed with a cork, to which adhere bits of thin metallic foil (fig. 4). Dimensions: height, 8 1/8 inches; diameter of base, 2 7/8 inches; diameter of neck (outside), 1 1/16 inches, (inside), 5/8 inch.

There are 12 whole bottles and fragments of several others in Subtype 1b, the bases of which have beveled edges. The bodies are cylindrical and 10 whole specimens are stamped near the base with the single marks: "L," "C," "S," "M," "I," and a backward "D." Fragments in this group display the markings: "X," "J," "W," "S(?)," "P," and "L(?)." The concave conical shoulder meets the body at a sharp juncture. All bottles of this group exhibit brandy neck finishes with a narrow ring beneath the collar and a thick lip curving slightly inward to the orifice. The stoppers are cork but there is no evidence of seals or wrappers (fig. 5). Dimensions: height, 7 5/8 inches; diameter of base, 2 13/16 inches; diameter of neck (outside), 1 inch, (inside), 5/8 inch.

Subtype 1c is similar in most respects to Subtype 1b, except for a different neck finish. This single bottle shows a wide slanting collar with a flaring ring beneath. The edges of both the collar and ring are sharply defined and the lip is very slightly curved. Near the base, an "S" is stamped in the body. The bottle is stoppered with a cork (fig. 6). Dimensions: height, 7 3/8 inches; diameter of base, 2 7/8 inches; diameter of neck (outside), 1 1/16 inches, (inside), 3/4 inch.

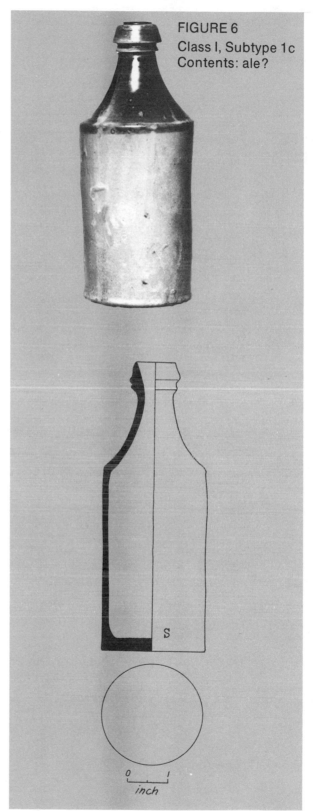

FIGURE 6
Class I, Subtype 1c
Contents: ale?

S

0   1
inch

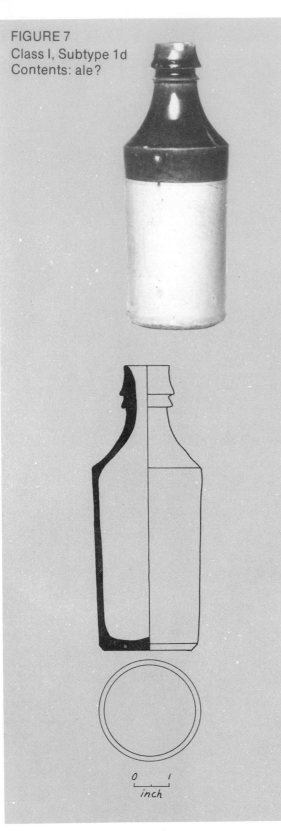

FIGURE 7
Class I, Subtype 1d
Contents: ale?

0   1
inch

Another one-of-a-kind item is the bottle which constitutes Subtype 1d. The shape of the base, body, and shoulder is like that of 1b and 1c, but the bottle is taller and the neck finish differs from 1b. The flared ring beneath the collar is not as close to the collar as in the previous types, and flares outward to a sharp edge. The collar is very wide, straight-sided at the mouth and flares outward and downward with a gentle concave curve. The bottle is stoppered with a cork and displays the remains of a thin foil wrapper on opposing sides of the collar (fig. 7). Dimensions: height, 7 15/16 inches; diameter of base, 2 7/8 inches; diameter of neck (outside), 1 3/16 inches, (inside), 11/16 inch.

Two bottles in Subtype 1e are the tallest of the glazed ceramic ale bottles. Some question remains as to whether these two bottles were a part of the cargo, or were intrusive—possibly left by early salvors. The top and bottom of one specimen was found on the stern deck, and the top and the bottom of the other specimen outside the gunwales at the bow (Jerome E. Petsche, 1972, personal communication). Their bodies are cylindrical with well defined, rounded shoulders and slightly conical necks. The neck finish is like that of Subtype 1a, except that the collar is wider and has a rounded lip. The orifice is sealed with its original cork and wire bail, and there are remnants of foil on the collar and neck. Stamped in the body at an angle, close to the beveled edge of the base, is: "PRICE/BRISTOL" (fig. 8). Dimensions: height, 9 3/4 inches; diameter of base, 3 1/2 inches; diameter of neck (outside), 1 inch, (inside), 5/8 inch.

Subtype 1f is represented by two bottles. They have flat bases with beveled edges, and cylindrical bodies which expand very slightly to the high rounded shoulders. The juncture between the shoulders and the conical necks is well defined. The collars have two grooves. The bottles had been sealed with corks, wire bails, and thin metal foil, remnants of which extended down some distance onto the necks (fig. 9). Dimensions: height, 7 1/2 inches; diameter of base, 3 inches; diameter of neck (outside), 7/8 inch, (inside), 5/8 inch.

One bottle has been classified as Subtype 1g. Similar morphologically to Type 1 and Subtype 1a, the major difference is in the neck finish which is grooved to form two rings and part of a third; the upper ring is the largest (fig. 10). A small "W" is stamped in the body near the base. Dimensions: height, 9 1/4 inches; diameter of base, 2 15/16 inches; diameter of neck (outside), 1 1/8 inches, (inside), 5/8 inch.

Class I, Type 2:

Twelve bottles of "Amsterdam Ale" were recovered from the hull of the *Bertrand*. These distinctive bottles are tall, wheel-turned, brown to reddish-brown unglazed stoneware (fig. 11). The base is flat with a slightly rounded edge. Near the base of the body is a half-inch-wide ridge. The cylindrical body is topped with rather smoothly curved shoulders and the short neck forms a concave ridge at its juncture with the shoulder. The remainder of the neck is cylindrical. The bottles are stoppered with corks covered by embossed thick foil caps which extend onto the necks. The relief stamped cap is circular with tiny dots forming its border. Within the border are the words "WYNAND FOCKINK / AMSTERDAM." At the very center of the cap is a nine-petalled flower. A thick, curving handle was applied high up on the shoulder and smoothed into the body and shoulder at its extremities. On the side of the bottle opposing the handle, just below the shoulder, an oval seal impressed into the body is composed of a lion wearing a crown. There also seems to be

FIGURE 8
Class I, Subtype 1e
Contents: ale

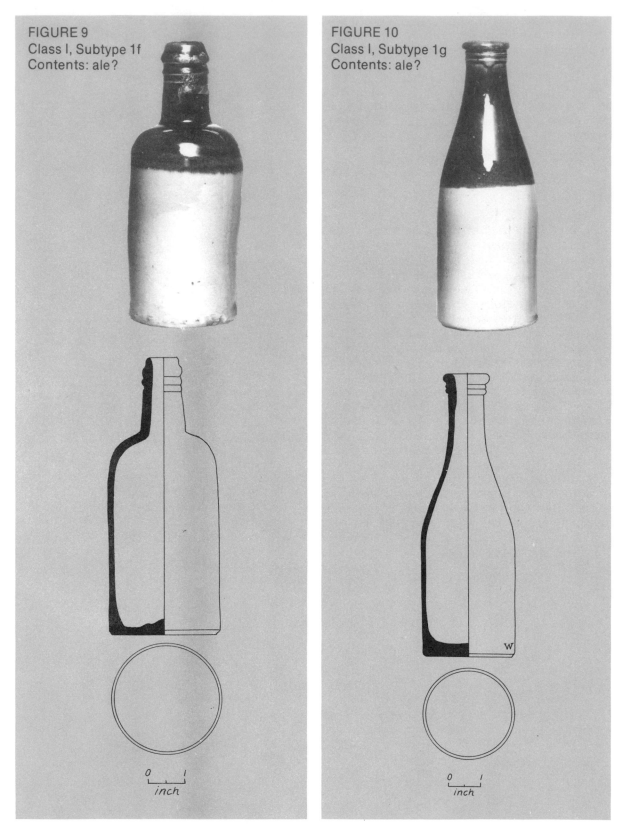

FIGURE 9
Class I, Subtype 1f
Contents: ale?

FIGURE 10
Class I, Subtype 1g
Contents: ale?

an abstract attempt to picture foliage around the figure. The central design element is surrounded by a shallow narrow groove, and the word "AMSTERDAMSCHE" (fig. 12). On this same side of the bottle, a little above the basal ridge, is imprinted the word "AMSTERDAM." Dimensions: height, 10 1/2 inches; diameter of base, 3 1/2 inches; diameter of neck (outside), 1 1/16 inches, (inside), sealed.

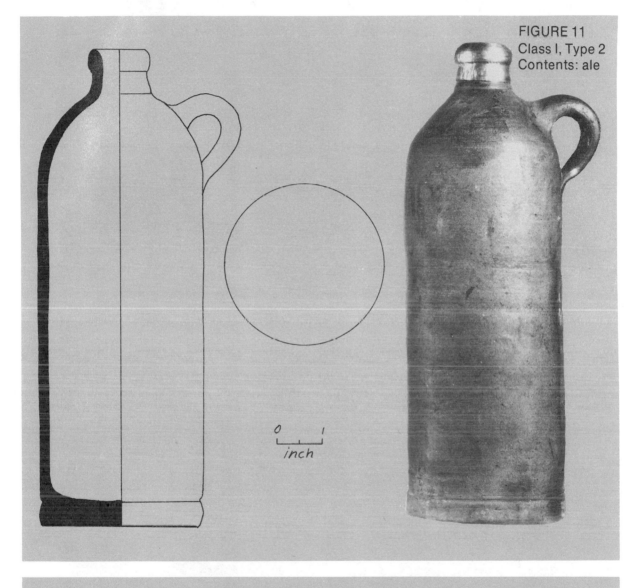

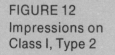

0   1
inch

FIGURE 11
Class I, Type 2
Contents: ale

FIGURE 12
Impressions on
Class I, Type 2

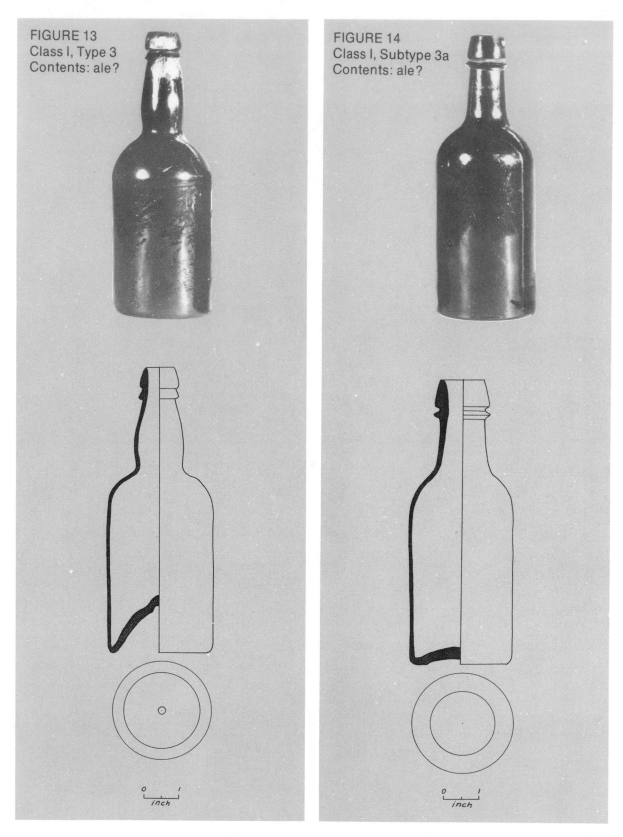

FIGURE 13
Class I, Type 3
Contents: ale?

FIGURE 14
Class I, Subtype 3a
Contents: ale?

Class I, Type 3, Subtypes 3a, 3b, 3c, 3d, 3e, 3f, 3g:

Nineteen whole amber glass bottles and a large number of fragments are represented here (Table 3). Type 3 bottles are similar in morphology to small brandy bottles (fig. 13). Rotated in three-piece molds, the bottles exhibit conically depressed bases with rounded edges, domed shoulders and brandy neck finishes. The greenish amber color is black in reflected light. Cork stoppers were held in place with wire bails. Dimensions: height, 8 1/8 inches; diameter of base, 3 inches; diameter of neck (outside), 7/8 inch, (inside), 11/16 inch.

Bottles designated as Subtype 3a (fig. 14) were blown in two-piece molds, but they are short and large in diameter for their height. They have a slanting collar-and-ring neck finish. The bottoms are plain with beveled edges and have slightly depressed centers. Dimensions: height, 8 inches; diameter of base, 2 13/16 inches; diameter of neck (outside), 1 inch, (inside), 13/16 inch.

Subtype 3b is distinguished by three-piece mold marks, a sloping collar finish without a ring, a bulbous neck, and a slightly dished base with a tiny nub at the center. The glass in all cases is so dark that it is black and opaque in reflected light (fig. 15). Dimensions: height, 8 5/8 inches; diameter of base, 2 9/16 inches; diameter of neck (outside), 1 inch, (inside), 3/4 inch.

Bottles of Subtype 3c are like those in Subtype 3b except they tend to be shorter. The base has a rounded edge and is quite deeply depressed. In addition, the neck has a brandy finish terminating in a flared ring at the base of the collar (fig. 16). Dimensions: height, 8 3/4 inches; diameter of base, 2 15/16 inches; diameter of neck (outside), 7/8 inch, (inside), 5/8 inch.

Morphologically, Subtype 3d bottles are like those in Class I, Type 4, except that they lack

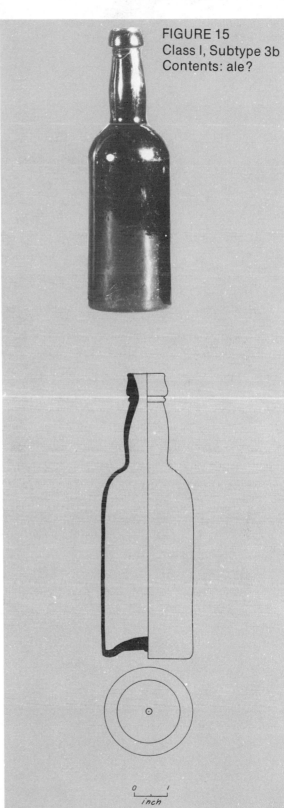

FIGURE 15
Class I, Subtype 3b
Contents: ale?

0   1
inch

FIGURE 16
Class I, Subtype 3c
Contents: ale?

0   1
inch

lettered embossing (fig. 17). The bottles are of the two-piece mold blown type, but tend to be somewhat asymmetrical. The collars are slightly flared and exhibit beveled-edged rings at the bases. The bottles have slightly depressed, plain basal concavities. Mold marks also are present on the bases. Dimensions: height, 9 7/16 inches; diameter of base, 2 1/2 inches; diameter of neck (outside), 1 1/16 inches, (inside) 11/16 inch.

Bottles of Subtype 3e have concave-sided collars with flared rings at their bases (fig.18). The necks are somewhat bulbous and the shoulders are gently rounded. The bottoms of these specimens have rounded edges and plain, slightly depressed centers. A tiny nub of glass appears in the center of the base. The bottles were blown in three-piece molds but tend to be somewhat asymmetrical and vary considerably in height. Dimensions: height, 8 7/8 inches; diameter of base, 2 3/4 inches; diameter of neck (outside), 15/16 inch, (inside), 3/4 inch.

Subtype 3f bottles (fig. 19) are very much like bottles of Subtype 3e but the necks tend to be shorter and more bulbous, and the basal depression is plain and deeply cupped. The neck finish tends to be more straight-sided. Dimensions: height, 8 5/8 inches; diameter of base, 2 11/16 inches; diameter of neck (outside), 1 inch, (inside) 3/4 inch.

The final Subtype 3g (fig. 20), looks like a half-size brandy bottle in all respects. These bottles exhibit a squat brandy shape with brandy neck finishes, and deeply depressed conical bases. Dimensions: height, 8 15/16 inches; diameter of base, 2 15/16 inches; diameter of neck (outside), 7/8 inch, (inside), 11/16 inch.

Class I, Type 4:

Only two amber glass bottles constitute Type 4, although several dozen additional bottles were found in direct association. It is almost certain that these two bottles contained ale (Table 3).

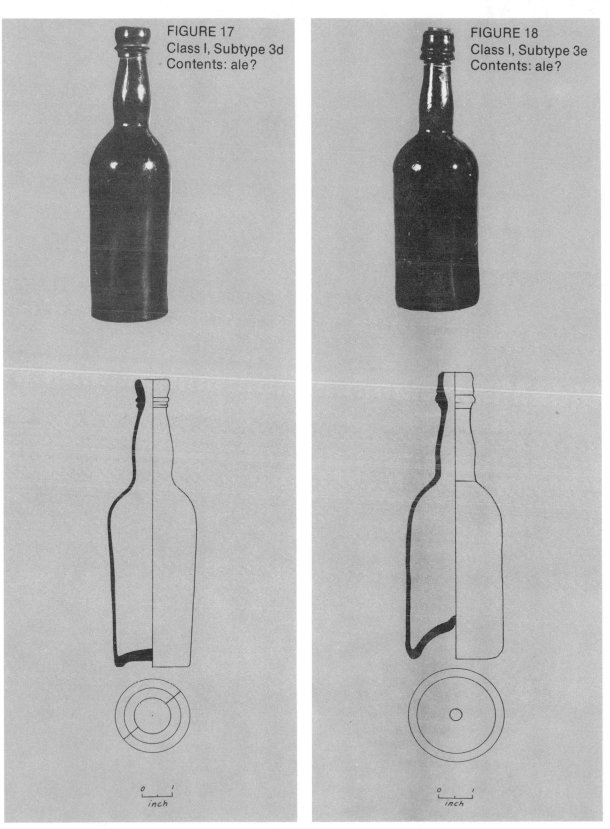

FIGURE 17
Class I, Subtype 3d
Contents: ale?

FIGURE 18
Class I, Subtype 3e
Contents: ale?

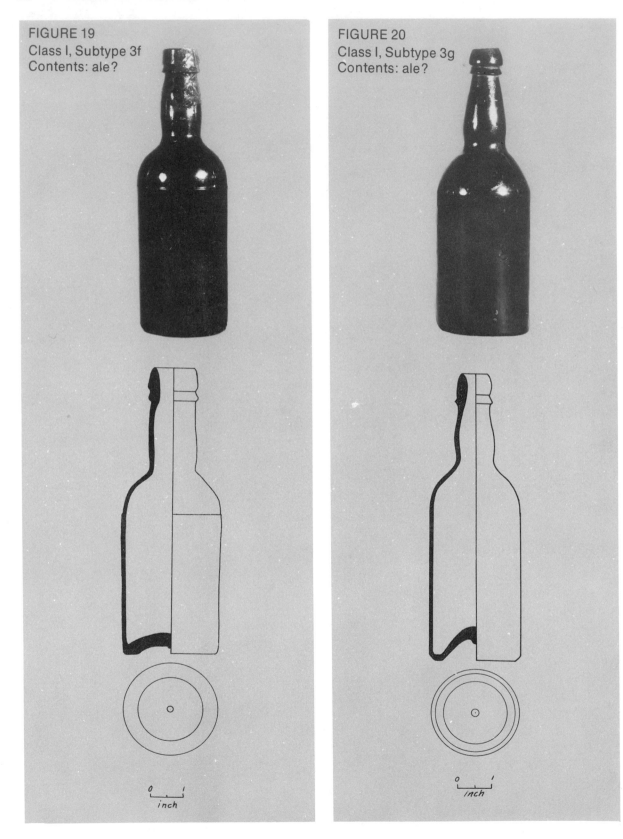

FIGURE 19
Class I, Subtype 3f
Contents: ale?

FIGURE 20
Class I, Subtype 3g
Contents: ale?

Type 4 ale bottles were blown in two-piece molds and exhibit a collar-and-ring brandy finish which permitted the corks to be securely wired in place (fig. 21). The edge of the base is flat, and the center of the base is a shallow dish-shaped depression. Blown letters on the bodies of the bottles read: "COOPER & CONGER / ST. LOUIS / ALE BREWERY." Remnants of thin silver-colored foil adhere to the corks and to the necks of these specimens. Nothing is known of Cooper and Conger St. Louis Ale Brewery despite a considerable research effort to document the company. Dimensions: height, 9 1/2 inches: diameter of base, 2 9/16 inches; diameter of neck (outside), 1 inch, (inside), 3/4 inch.

FIGURE 21
Class I, Type 4
Contents: ale

CLASS III
WINE, WHISKEY, BITTERS, AND OTHER INTOXICANTS

Class III, Type 1, Subtype 1a:

Only three examples of this type are present in the collection (Table 4). Two of the bottles are transparent, non-lead, aqua-colored glass demijohns with cork stoppers (figs. 22, 23). Only one of the bottles is wicker covered. Both contain a deep red wine, possibly of French origin. Dimensions: height, 18 inches; diameter of base, 7 1/2 inches; diameter of neck (outside), 1 5/8 inches, (inside), 7/8 inch.

Although the third demijohn has roughly the same capacity as the former examples, it differs in height, color, and diameter of the base, and is classified in Subtype 1a. Originally it had a wicker cover, but was so fragmented that it could not be recovered intact (Jerome E. Petsche, 1972, personal communication). All three demijohns exhibit asymmetrical qualities and pontil scars, indicating that they were free-blown. Nothing has survived of information pertaining to the manufacturer, wholesaler or consignee of these vessels or their contents. Dimensions: height, approximately 17 1/2 inches; diameter of base, 7 5/8 inches; diameter of neck (outside), 1 9/16 inches, (inside), 1 1/4 inches.

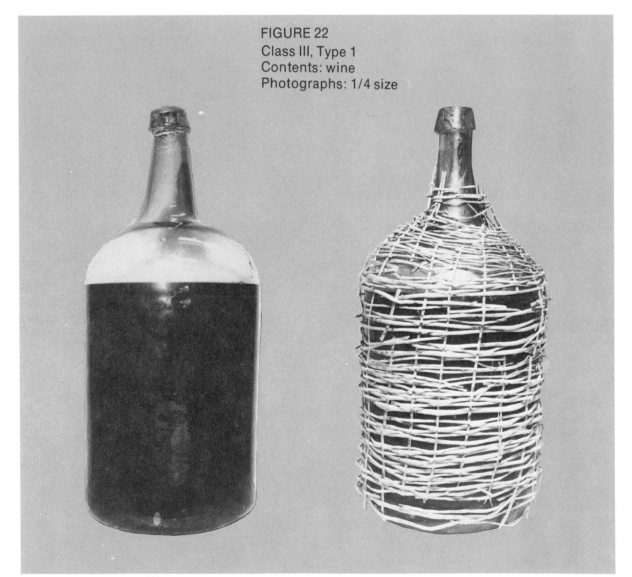

FIGURE 22
Class III, Type 1
Contents: wine
Photographs: 1/4 size

CLASS III, Type 2, Subtypes 2a, 2b, 2c, 2d:

All of the thick green glass champagne bottles are blown-in-mold types, and were rotated in the molds while the glass was still molten (Table 4). The bottles in Type 2 exhibit high basal kick-ups with convex knobs at the centers (figs. 24a, b; 27a). Dimensions: height, 11 15/16 inches; diameter of base, 3 11/16 inches; diameter of neck (outside), 15/16 inch, (inside), 3/4 inch.

Those bottles in Subtype 2a are the same except that they lack convex knobs at the centers of the kick-ups. The wine finish on all of the bottles was produced with the aid of a lipping tool. Dimensions: height, 12 3/8 inches; diameter of base, 3 3/4 inches; diameter of neck (outside), 1 1/8 inches, (inside), 13/16 inch.

Two types of stoppers and seals are associated with the champagne bottles. At least 89

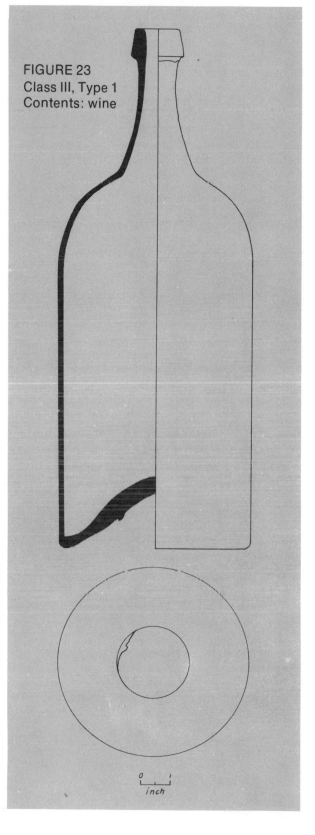

FIGURE 23
Class III, Type 1
Contents: wine

0   1
inch

bottles exhibit mushroom-shaped corks held in place with opposed metal clamps (fig. 25). The corks are covered with a very thin, gold-colored foil wrapper which extends down the neck nearly to the shoulder. The second, and larger groups of bottles (ca. 113) have mushroom-shaped corks held in place by knotless string ties (fig. 26) over the tops of which, at right angles, are twisted wire bails. Thick lead foil seals or caps cover the corks and extend down a short distance onto the necks of the bottles. The foil caps for these bottles

and for some of those in Subtype 2b exhibit four variations of relief stamping as depicted double size in figures 28-31.

Wooden cases associated with the champagne bottles were marked as follows:

1. Bottles with clamped cork stoppers: "E.V.H. /PRINCE IMPERIAL."
2. Bottles with string ties and wire bails: "IMPERIAL."
3. Bottles without corks and seals: "CHAMPAGNE / VeP & C⁰ 76 / MIS_____/ M_____."

FIGURE 24
Class III, Type 2
Contents: champagne
Photographs: 1/2 size

a   b

4. At least one crate of champagne is known to have been lettered "1 DOZ. QTS. / CHAMPAGNE / J.W.B. / N.Y. / CIDER / DEPOT 92 & 94 CEDAR ST." on one end, but the nature of the associated bottles is unknown.

It would appear that at least some of the champagne was exported from Rheims, France, and was wholesaled by a St. Louis, Missouri, firm. Piper Heidseick champagnes are still being produced and exported for sale in the United States. They are considered premium quality wines.

For lack of a better term, the 12 1/2-ounce bottles in Subtype 2b are designated as "splits," since the contents are about one-half the volume of the preceding type. These are of the blown-in-mold variety, and no mold marks are visible except on Subtype 2d. Each bottle has a high kick-up in its base, but at the centers of some of the bases (Subtype 2c) the convex knob is absent. Dimensions, Subtype 2b: height, 9 3/4 inches; diameter of base, 3 inches; diameter of neck (outside), 13/16 inch, (inside), 3/4 inch. Dimensions, Subtype 2c: height, 9 1/4 inches; diameter of base, 3 inches; diameter of neck (outside), 13/16 inch, (inside), 3/4 inch. Dimensions, Subtype 2d: height, 9 1/4 inches; diameter of base, 2 15/16 inches; diameter of neck (outside), 13/16 inch, (inside), 3/4 inch.

Subtypes 2b and 2c have mushroom-shaped corks, held in place with knotless string ties and twisted wire bails, but there is considerable variation in cork markings, seals and case marks, as noted below:

1. Thick gray-white putty-like coating over the cork, extending onto the neck (99 bottles). Case marks: "GREEN SEAL"; *consignee:* "VIVIAN & SIMPSON/ VIRGINIA CITY, M.T."

2. Thick, hard, blue-stained cellulose coating over cork, extending onto the shoulder (81 bottles). Case marks: "GREEN SEAL."

3. Thin gold-colored foil wrapper over cork, extending onto neck (385 bottles). Cork marks: Five point star at center of end surrounded by the letters "DE____VE 8 /_____NC /_____SF / _____CIE." Stem of cork lettered "VINNO / FRANCE / IMPERIAL."

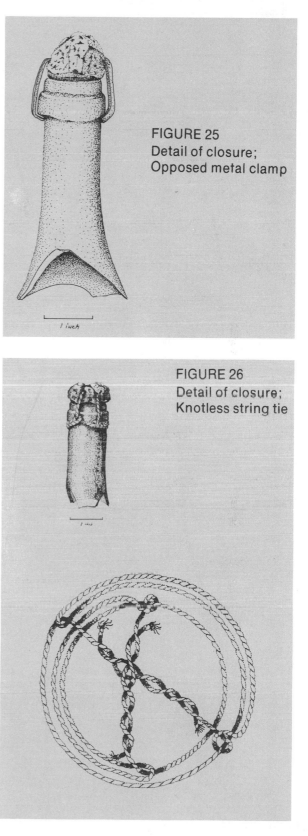

FIGURE 25
Detail of closure;
Opposed metal clamp

FIGURE 26
Detail of closure;
Knotless string tie

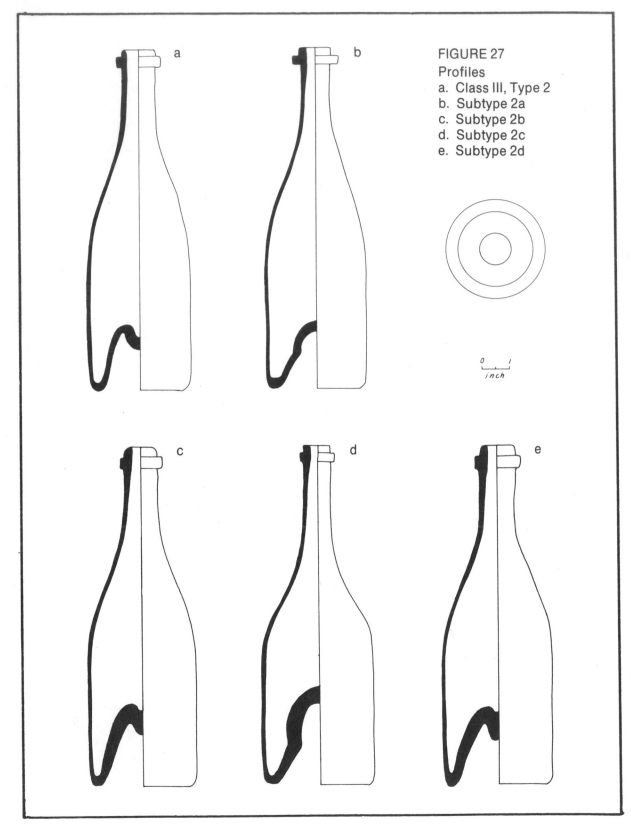

FIGURE 27
Profiles
a. Class III, Type 2
b. Subtype 2a
c. Subtype 2b
d. Subtype 2c
e. Subtype 2d

FIGURE 28. *Relief stamping around the border of the cap represents a rope inside of which are the words "HEIDSEICK & Co./REIMS. The outer relief-stamped rope is broken by the word "DUPREE." The center of the seal exhibits a cluster of grapes and four leaves surrounded by a raised twisted cord.*

FIGURE 29. *This seal is relief stamped around the border "H. PIPER & Co./*RHEIMS*." The center of the seal exhibits a cluster of grapes and three leaves, surrounded by a twisted cord broken by the word "DUPREE." The stars before and after "RHEIMS" are six-pointed.*

FIGURE 30. *This variation is similar to that depicted in figure 29, except that the "H" in "H. PIPER & Co." is hooked on the left side to form a "J."*

FIGURE 31. *This seal is also similar to that depicted in figure 29. Exceptions included the leaves which are marked with three small circles, dots instead of stars before and after "RHEIMS," and the absence of the word "DUPREE."*

FIGURE 32. *Mark appearing on the bottoms of corks in bottles of Class III, Subtypes 2b and 2c.*

FIGURE 33. *Artist's reconstruction from remnants of paper labels on bottles of Class III, Subtypes 2b and 2c.*

Case marks: "IMPERIAL"; "FRANCE /_____/ IMPERIAL"; "St. LOUIS."

4. Thick lead foil seal bearing relief stamped design and letters as in number 2, above (102 bottles).
5. Corks are present, but the nature of the seals is unknown. Cork marks: a crown with a circle around it (fig. 32).

A number of bottles which exhibit thick stamped foil seals also display remnants of paper labels. These were lettered in black and gold on a white background to read: "LE MARQUIS DE PONCET / CHAMPAGNE / MOUSSEUX /_____AYQU / SOL_____E_____" (fig. 33).

One major reason for believing that Bertrand champagne bottles were mold made is that Subtype 2d is like Subtype 2b except it bears the marks of a three-piece mold. Represented by one specimen, this bottle (fig. 34) exhibits the foil seal of Piper Heidseick Company.

At least one container which held wine bottles in the cargo was marked "AMERICAN WINE Co. / SPARKLING / CATAWBA / ST. LOUIS, MO." on one end; the top of the crate was stenciled "VIVIAN & SIMPSON / VIRGINIA CITY, M.T.." Unfortunately, no information appears in the field notes to indicate the size and nature of the bottles in the container. In addition, according to the field notes, some of the wine and champagne bottles were packed in thin-walled wooden barrels and peck-size wicker baskets.

Class III, Type 3:

Evidence exists for at least 24 bottles of imported French wine in the cargo. All Type 3 bottles are transparent olive green in color and all are free-blown with high basal kick-ups and wine neck finishes. (Table 5). The basal depressions are marked by convex knobs at the centers. Dimensions: height, 11 1/2 inches; diameter of base, 2 7/8 inches; diameter of neck (outside), 1 1/8 inches, (inside), 7/8 inch.

The capacity of these tall, handsome bottles, when filled to the brim, is 25 1/2 ounces and all were stoppered with cylindrical wine corks covered with stamped foil seals (fig. 35). The seals are of two types, the first of which exhibits a border of raised dots and central design composed of a coat-of-arms. Raised letters to the left of the central design read "ARMES DE," and those on the right read "BORDEAUX" (fig. 36a). This seal was found associated with eight whole bottles and fragments of five others.

The second type of seal was found affixed to 11 wine bottles. It bears a raised dot border, inside of which appear letters reading "L. MERIC AINE / BORDEAUX." The center of the seal is plain, but defined by a raised line (fig. 36b). Nothing is known of the container in which the wine bottles were shipped.

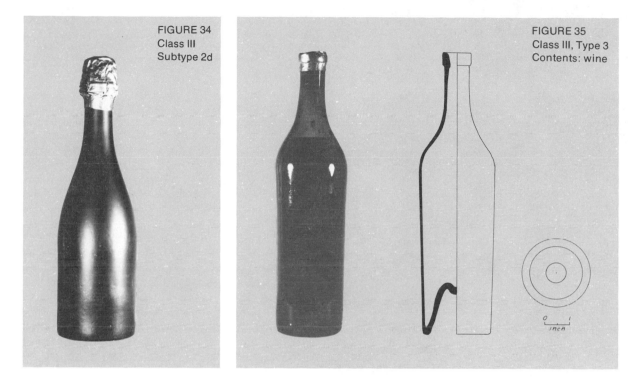

FIGURE 34
Class III
Subtype 2d

FIGURE 35
Class III, Type 3
Contents: wine

Class III, Type 4, Subtypes 4a, 4b, 4c:

Only two 12-bottle cases of bourbon whiskey, with an average alcohol content of 24 percent, were found in the *Bertrand* cargo (Table 5). These 25-ounce amber and dark green bottles are of the blown-in-mold type (three-piece molds) with slanting collar-and-ring finishes (figs. 37, 38a, b, c). The flat outer edge of the base on each bottle is plain, but the center of the base is dished and bears a small nub at the center. The edge of the base on Subtype 4a is relief stamped "WILLINGTON GLASS WORKS," and the 'N' in "WILLINGTON" and the 'S's' in "GLASS" are backwards. The edge of the base of Subtype 4b is lettered "ELLENVILLE GLASS WORKS." Dimensions, Type 4: height, 11 1/2 inches; diameter of base, 3 1/16 inches; diameter of neck (outside), 1 inch, (inside), 3/4 inch. Dimensions, Subtype 4a: height, 11 15/16 inches; diameter of base, 3 1/8 inches; diameter of neck (outside), 1 inch, (inside), 3/4 inch. Dimensions, Subtype 4b: height, 11 3/8 inches; diameter of base, 3 1/8 inches; diameter of neck (outside), 1 inch, (inside), 7/8 inch.

The cases in which the bottles were shipped are marked as follows: "BOURBON / WHIS-KEY / COCKTAIL"; *consignee:* "WORDEN & CO / HELL GATE."

Another case of 12 amber bottles made in three-piece molds, which closely resemble those in Type 4, were found in the Bertrand hold. These have been designated as Subtype 4c (fig. 38c). The body of each bottle is cylindrical, with a long tapering neck terminating in a slanting collar oil finish. The rounded shoulder bears the raised letters "PATENTED," and the recessed base is lettered "W. M^cCULLY & Co / PITTS BURGH PA." The center of the base bears three small raised dots. The alcoholic content of the liquid in these 21 1/2-ounce bottles was only 4 1/2 percent and could not be identified generically. What was left of the shipping crate was marked "G. P. DORRIS / VIRGINIA CITY." Dimensions, Subtype 4c: height, 10 15/16 inches; diameter of base, 2 13/16 inches; diameter of neck, (outside), 1 inch, (inside), 3/4 inch.

Class III, Type 5

There are 18 bottles in the Bertrand collection which contained brandy (fig. 39). They were blown in three-piece molds and bear the

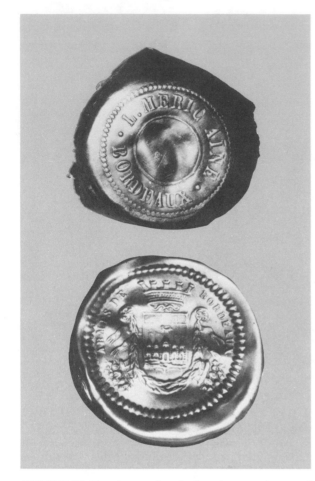

FIGURE 36. Two types of seals found on specimens of Class III, Type 3. Photographs: double size.

typical double ring or brandy neck finish (Table 5). The 24-ounce bottles are stoppered with corks held in place with twisted copper wire bails, covered with thin silver-colored metallic foil wrappers extending onto the necks. The bases have rounded edges and bear deep conical shaped kickups. The contents are 6 percent alcohol by volume.

Several of the bottle corks bear the stem markings "E &_____/ _____ND," and "F. & G. HIBBERT / LONDON."

The wooden cases for the bottles are marked as follows: "12 QT. / BRANDY COCK TAIL / FROM: C.A. RICHARDS / 91 WASHINGTON ST. / BOSTON"; "GLASS / WITH CARE / STUART & Co. / DEER LODGE." Presumably the brandy was bottled and exported by F. and G. Hibbert of London and retailed by C. A. Richards of Boston to Stuart and Company of Deer Lodge in Montana Territory. Dimensions, Type 5: height, 9 13/16 inches, diameter of base, 3 11/16 inches; diameter of neck (outside), 1 inch, (inside), 3/4 inch.

Class III, Type 6, Subtypes 6a, 6b, 6c, 6d, 6e, 6f:

The dark amber and dark green Hostetter's bitters bottles represent the largest single category of bottles with alcoholic contents (Table 6). One hundred and ninety-one, 12-bottle cases of Hostetter's bitters in two sizes of bottles have been counted in the collection. The average alcohol content is 27 percent by volume, which is somewhat greater than the original Hostetter formula.

The small, amber, 22-ounce bottles in Type 6 were blown in two-piece molds and have slanting collar neck finishes (fig. 40). Bottle bases are flat and exhibit shallow dish-shaped depressions at the centers. Some of the bases have relief marks which are depicted in Figure 41. Apparently, the "L&W" mark should be attributed to the Lorenz and Wightman firm who operated the Pittsburgh Glass Works.

Type 6 bottles are embossed on one side with the inscription "DR. J. HOSTETTER'S / STOMACH BITTERS," and were stoppered with corks. The bottles also display fragments of paper labels on two sides. These are described below with Subtype 6a. Dimensions, Type 6: height, 8 7/8 inches; base, 2 5/8 by 2 5/8 inches; diameter of neck (outside), 1 1/8 inches, (inside), 3/4 inh.

Bitters bottles in the Subtype 6a category are dark green or amber in color and are similar morphologically to Type 6 except that they have a greater capacity of about 28 ounces. Relief marks on the bases of the bottles are shown in Figure 42. Profiles of Subtypes 6a and b are depicted in Figure 43.

The bottles contain cork stoppers, covered with thick foil seals. Over the tops of the seals are proprietary revenue stamps (fig. 44a, b). A dark blue paper label with gold (now gray) print was affixed to one side of a bottle and the opposing side displayed a label with black print on a white background. The upper half of the black and white label depicts St. George slaying the dragon. Dimensions, Subtype 6a: height, 9 5/16 inches; base, 2 3/16 by 2 3/16 inches; diameter of neck (outside), 1 1/16 inch, (inside), 3/4 inch.

One of the gold-lettered blue paper labels, reconstructed from several fragments, reads as follows:

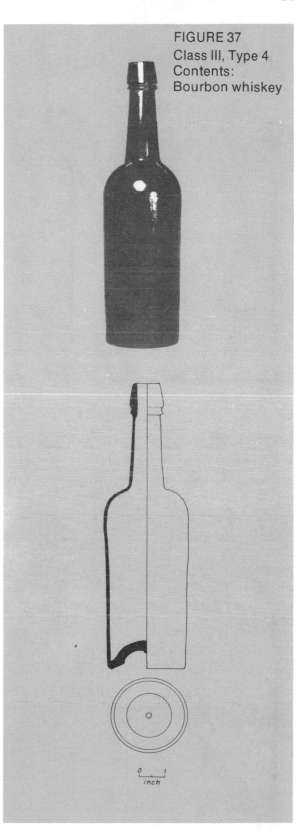

FIGURE 37
Class III, Type 4
Contents:
Bourbon whiskey

HOSTETTER'S
CELEBRATED
STOMACH
BITTERS

One wine-glassful taken three times a day before meals, will be a swift and certain cure for Dyspepsia, Liver Complaint, and every species of indigestion - an unfailing remedy for Intermittent Fever, Fever and Ague, and all kinds of periodical flux, Colics, and Choleric maladies - a cure for costiveness - a mild and safe invigorant and corroborant for delicate females - a good, anti-bilious, alternative and tonic preparation for ordinary family purposes - a powerful recuperant after the frame has been reduced and altered by sickness - an excellent appetizer as well as a strengthener of the blood and other fluids desirable as a corrective and mild cathartic and an agreeable and wholesome stimulant.

Persons in a debilitated state should commence by taking small doses and increase with their strength.

0   1
inch

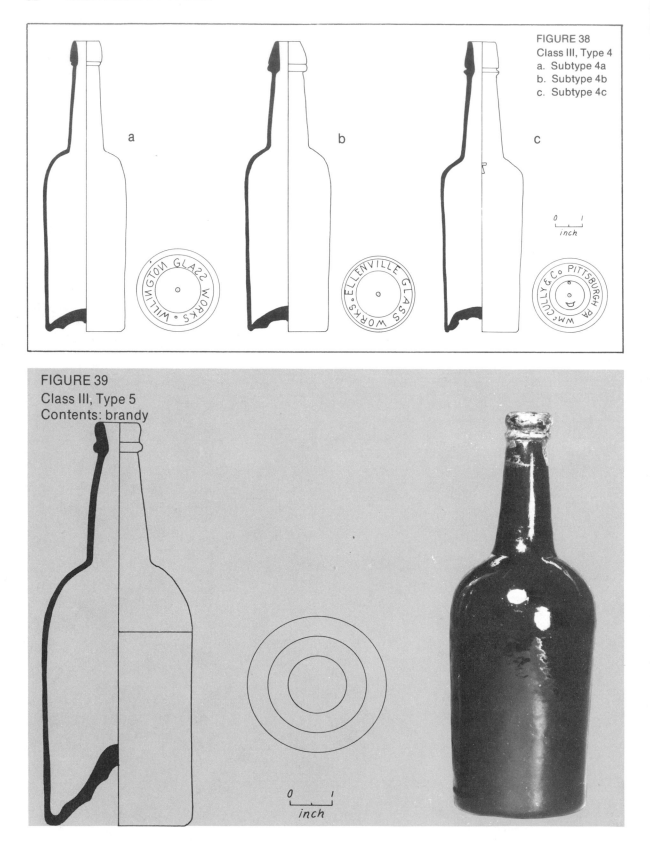

FIGURE 38
Class III, Type 4
a. Subtype 4a
b. Subtype 4b
c. Subtype 4c

FIGURE 39
Class III, Type 5
Contents: brandy

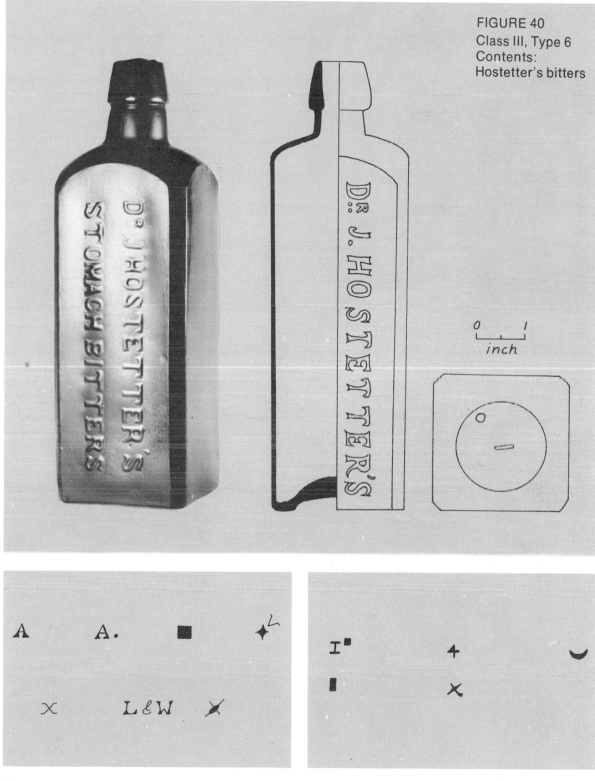

FIGURE 40
Class III, Type 6
Contents:
Hostetter's bitters

Figure 41. Relief marks on bottoms of bottles in Class III, Type 6.

FIGURE 42. Relief marks on bottoms of bottles in Class III, Subtype 6a.

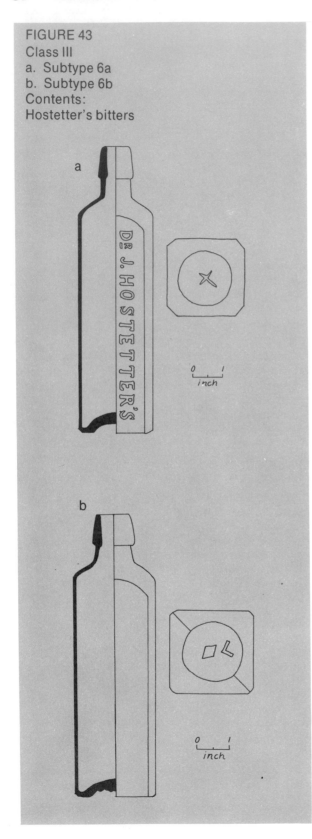

FIGURE 43
Class III
a. Subtype 6a
b. Subtype 6b
Contents:
Hostetter's bitters

One group of eight large plain Hostetter's bottles were recovered with four embossed specimens in a crate marked: "HOSTETTERS / STOMACH / BITTERS / BAR STORES / BERTRAND." The dark green and amber bottles, designated as Subtype 6b have no raised letters on their sides, but otherwise they are like the bottles in Subtype 6a. Dimensions, Subtype 6b: height, 9 3/4 inches; base, 2 7/8 by 2 7/8 inches; diameter of neck (outside), 1 1/16 inch, (inside), sealed.

Larger Hostetter's bottles are definitely in the minority, and, at this writing, no more than two cases have been found. Perhaps others will come to our attention as work progresses in opening the crates.

Wooden Hostetter's cases bear metal straps at the corners, and the boxes are marked in black stenciling in the following manner: "HOSTETTER & SMITH / SOLE / MANU-FACTURERS / &/ PROPRIETORS / PITTS-BURGH, P.A."; *consignee:* "VIVIAN & SIMPSON / VIRGINIA CITY, M.T.." Inside many of the cases were eight almanacs (fig. 45) packed in sets of two, or twelve almanacs packed in four sets of three. Over the almanacs large folded Hostetter broadsides had been placed, one per box. The broadsides are lettered in bold reddish-brown print, and at the center of each is a woodcut in black of St. George slaying the dragon. Unfortunately, not one complete broadside has been recovered. Fragments pieced together in the Bertrand Conservation Laboratory indicate that they measured 18 by 24 1/2 inches.

There are eight 32-ounce bottles of J. H. Schroeder's Bitters in the Bertrand cargo and a number of fragments assigned to Subtype 6c (fig. 46). The contents of the whole bottles averaged 25 percent alcohol by volume. These olive green bottles were blown in two-piece molds and the slanted collar neck finish was applied with a lipping tool. The "French Square" bottles have beveled corners and are stoppered with corks, capped with red sealing wax or a tan colored putty-like substance. The edge of the base of each bottle is flat and the center bears a plain, shallow, circular dish-shaped depression. Three sides of the body are plain; the fourth bears the relief molded words "J. H. SCHROEDER / 28 WALL STREET / LOUISVILLE, KY." Dimensions, Subtype 6c: height, 9 15/16 inches; base, 3 1/16 by 3 1/16 inches; diameter of neck (outside), 1 inch, (inside), 3/4 inch.

At least two of the plain sides bore black-on-white paper labels with chain-like borders. As much as could be reconstructed from fragments of two labels appears below and in Figure 47:

HOSTETTER & SMITH
Sole Proprietors and Manufacturers
58, 59 & 60 Water & Front Sts. Pittsburgh, Pa.

In order to guard against counterfeits, purchasers will please observe the name Dr. J. Hostetter's Stomach Bitters pressed on the Bottle and our Proprietory Revenue Stamp covering the cork and see that our autograph signature (to counterfeit which is a felony) is on the label.

...awba Wines ...
... Old B
... in ...
...act, an ...
...sso...
... the social ...
...am ...
... he ta...
therefore I d...
also give a few ...
   The invaluabl... e...
was inherited by ... proprie...
great-grandfather ...cupied the ...
assistant bar-keeper on board the ...
He has a great ca-ere, not only...
the "cuisine," but also a cute judge of ...
human nature in the spirit line, and it may ...
sumed that the liberal distribution of his in...
BITTERs among the noble immigrants cheered ...
souls to face the dangers and privations duri...
long, dreary voyage, and also endowed them w...
steadiness of habit and gait which enabled t...
wards to stand so admirably firm on Plymou...
   The ingredients necessary for accomp...
quasi "Balm of Gilead" are gathered and ...
special agents and trustworthy students of ...
all the different zones of our globe. F...
land to Cape Horn, on OUR continent; from ...
clad mountains of the Himalaya to the sunny ...
the Grampian Hills, and "all intermediate h...
on the as yet unannexed portion of the balan...
world, contributions are levied of their choic...
most fragrant flowers, roots, herbs, and spices, ...
fect ...renial liquid.
   ... and several other eminent "Professors," have ...
submitted said decoction to the most searching chem...
cal analysis, and the result of our united labor proved
(and "all the Doctors agreed") that my production is
neither "narcotic" nor "drastic"—entirely free from all
deleterious substances, and, therefore ...fect "triumph of science in the BITTER line;" ... as such, I recommend it.
   The public are invited to call and taste ... above BITTERs at ... Wall Street, Citizens and strangers ...
may fi... inconvenient to come ...y store can sa...

FIGURE 44. Proprietary revenue stamps, Class III, Type 6.

ple the same at the Galt H... ...isville Hotel ...
Charles, Capitol, Hotel ... Hudson, Hall ...
United States Hotel Sa... ...ational Wal ...
tal Palace, S...toga, and at all other well ...
in the city and on the rive...
   A liberal discount will be ...
will find it profitable to keep ...
BITTERs on hand.
   ☞ Indigent sick who may ...ong...
smile ... something good ... will ... furnis...
always ... they do ... complain of ...
      ...H SCHROEDE...

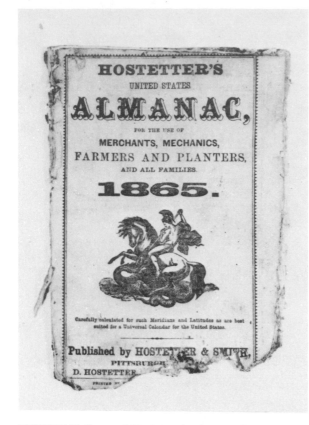

FIGURE 45. Cover of Hostetter's almanac found in cases of bitters.

The 12-bottle shipping crates are stenciled in black as follows: "J. H. SCHROEDER'S / STOMACH / BITTERS / LOUISVILLE, KY."; "SCHROEDER'S / BITTERS"; "_____/ CARE / J. J. ROE & CO / ST. LOUIS / MO."

One case of 12 dark green, square bitters bottles of two kinds were recovered from the hold of the *Bertrand*. Eleven 26-ounce bottles assigned to Subtype 6d (fig. 48) are morphologically like the others in Type 6 except that one side is lettered vertically in raised letters to read: "C. S. KINTZING / ST. LOUIS MO." Both Subtype 6d bottles and the single specimen assigned to Subtype 6e are so dark in reflected light that they look black in color. The 6e bottle is slightly taller than the bottles in Subtype 6d, and all four sides are plain; there are no marks whatsoever on this specimen. Dimensions, Subtype 6d: height, 8 7/8 inches; base, 2 13/16 by 2 13/16 inches; diameter of neck (outside), 1 inch, (inside), 11/16 inch. Dimensions, Subtype 6e: height, 9

3/4 inches; diameter of base, 2 7/8 inches; diameter of neck (outside), 1 inch, (inside), 3/4 inch.

Inasmuch as the contents of these bottles average 25 percent alcohol by volume, they are assumed to be bitters. The case in which they were shipped is marked in black stencil as follows: "1 DOZ"; *consignee:* "STUART & Cº / DEER LODGE."

Only 48 14-ounce bottles of Udolphowolfe's Aromatic Schnapps were represented in the *Bertrand* cargo, the alcohol content of which averages almost 21 percent by volume. Essentially these Subtype 6f French Squares are of the Hostetter type, green in color with relief molded letters on three sides reading "UDOLPHOWOLFE'S / AROMATIC SCHNAPPS / SCHIEDAM" (fig. 49). Dimensions, Subtype 6f: height, 8 1/16 inches; base, 2 3/8 by 2 3/8 inches; diameter of neck (outside), 1 inch, (inside), 3/4 inch.

The cork-stoppered slanting collared bottles were packed twelve to a case. Case ends are stenciled: "UDOLPHOWOLFE'S CELEBRATED SCHIEDAM SCHNAPPS / 2 DOZ. PINTS / STUART & CO. / DEER LODGE," and "WOLFE'S CELEBRATED SCHIEDAM SCHNAPPS / 2 DOZ. PINTS / STUART & CO. / DEER LODGE." According to Wilson (1974) "Udolpho Wolfe's Son & Co." used a label on their bottles bearing the trademark "DIAMOND W.A.S. LABEL," but none are recorded for the Bertrand specimens.

Class III, Type 7:

To Type 7 have been assigned 109 nearly square, amber-colored, cabin-shaped bottles containing Drake's Plantation Bitters (fig. 50) and an additional number of fragments (Table 7). The 24 bottles tested contain nearly 17 percent alcohol. The front and reverse sides of the bottles have six relief logs above plain panels which accomodated paper labels. The tiered roof shoulder on the front side is embossed with letters on all three tiers as follows: top: "S T / DRAKES"; middle: "1860 / PLANTATION"; bottom: "X / BITTERS." The middle tier of the reverse side is embossed: "PATENTED / 1862." The two remaining sides are molded to represent logs, which cross at the corners of the bottles, and the tiered roof above is corrugated. The necks are cylindrical and terminate in slanting collar finishes. On each bottle the edge of the base is flat and the center of the base bears a plain dished depression. All of these specimens were stoppered with corks.

In many instances fragments of black-on-white paper labels were found adhering to the front and back panels. Some bottles show evidence of having been wrapped in a black-and-white printed paper wrapper bearing testimony of the effectiveness of the tonic.

Wooden shipping cases for Drake's Plantation Bitters are unusual in that the lids of several exhibit single strength glass display panels or advertisements attached to the inner side (fig. 51). Each sign is composed with a black border surrounding a large white oval trimmed with gold. The central oval is lettered in three different letter styles; the top line of letters are gold outlined in black, the middle line of letters in red outlined in gold and black, and the bottom line in gold letters outlined in black.

The cases bear the following stenciled marks on the exteriors: "DRAKE'S PLANTATION BITTERS / DEPOT NEW YORK," or "S T 1860 X / G / G T O & S / WITH CARE VIA SARNIA"; *consignees:* "WORDEN & CO / HELL GATE, M.T.," or "VIVIAN & SIMPSON / VIRGINIA CITY, M.T." Dimensions, Type 7: height, 9 7/8 inches; base, 2 3/4 by 2 3/4 inches; diameter of neck (outside), 1 1/16 inches, (inside), 13/16 inch.

Class III, Type 8:

All bottles in this type contain 25 ounces of 23 proof Kelly's Old Cabin Bitters and are molded to represent log cabins (fig. 52). The front and back sides bear three mold-impressed windows and a door. Corrugated roof panels which form the shoulders on the front and back are embossed: "KELLYS / OLD CABIN / BITTERS." The remaining two sides bear plain panels for labels, topped with five relief logs and a triangular-shaped space under the pitch of the roof embossed: "PATENTED / 1863." The bottle necks are cylin-

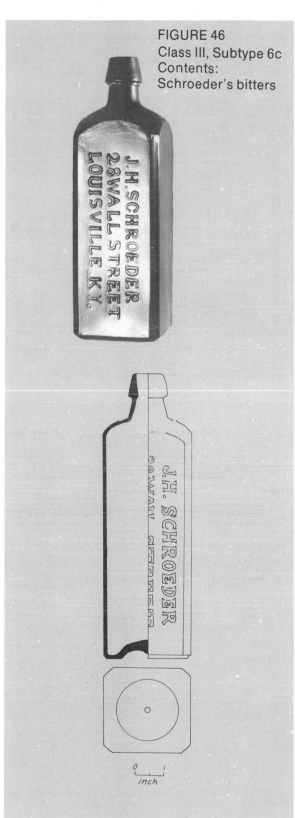

FIGURE 46
Class III, Subtype 6c
Contents:
Schroeder's bitters

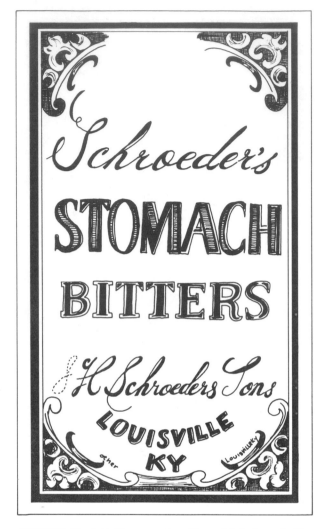

FIGURE 47. Artist's reconstruction of label on J. H. Schroeder's bitters bottle.

drical, terminating in slanting collar neck finishes. Bases are flat at the periphery, but the centers exhibit plain shallow dish-shaped depressions. All of the bottles are sealed with corks. Several bottles exhibited fragments of black-on-white paper labels printed by the American Bank Note Company of New York (fig. 53).

Kelly's bitters crates show some variation in stenciling; two consignees and one retailer are represented. The stencils appear as follows: "KELLEY'S / OLD CABIN BITTERS / DEPOTS NEW YORK & ST. LOUIS" (fig. 54), sides: (red) eight point sunburst with a letter at the base of each ray, lettered: "O L D / C A B I N." At the center of the sunburst appears the date "1863". Some cases have no marks on their sides. Tops: "GLASS WEIGHT / THIS SIDE UP WITH CARE / G. P. DORRIS / VIRGINIA CITY / MONTANA, TY."; or, "WORDEN AND CO. / HELL GATE"; or, "FROM / H. A. RICHARDS / WASHINGTON / 57, / BOSTON / GIN COCKTAIL / WORDEN AND CO. / HELL GATE.; Dimensions, Type 8: height, 9 1/8 inches; base, 2 3/4 by 3 7/16 inches; diameter of neck (outside), 1 inch, (inside), 3/4 inch.

Class III. Type 9, Subtype 9a:

At this time there are 69 so-called "leg bottles" containing Schroeder's Spice Bitters catalogued in the collection (Table 7). The contents include 44 percent alcohol. These 28-ounce dark amber bottles appear to have been blown in two-piece molds and are finished with a single ring wine finish. The basal edges are rounded, but the bases themselves consist of fairly shallow, dish-shaped depressions with tiny nubs at their centers. Relief molded lettering on the bodies of the bottles reads: "SCHROEDER'S / SPICE / BITTERS" (fig. 56). Apparently, judging from recorded fragments, a 3 by 5 inch black-on-white paper label was affixed to each bottle below the raised letters on the side.

The bottles are packed 12 to a case and the case lumber bears one of three stencils as follows: " ⬦R⬦ / CARE / J.J. ROE & CO / ST. LOUIS / MO. / 2 & 2"; "J. H. SCHROEDER'S / COCK-TAIL / BITTERS / LOUISVILLE, KY."; "SCHROEDER'S COCK TAIL / BITTERS." Dimensions, Type 9: height, 11 15/16 inches; diameter of base, 3 3/8 inches; diameter of neck (outside), 1 1/16 inches, (inside), 3/4 inch.

Only one bottle of Subtype 9a was found in the cargo. Morphologically it is like the bottles in Type 9 except that it exhibits no raised lettering, it has mold marks from a three-piece mold, and shows considerable evidence of work at the collar with a lipping tool. It is deep amber in color. Dimensions, Subtype 9a:

height, 11 3/4 inches; diameter of base, 3 1/2 inches; diameter of neck (outside), 1 1/8 inches, (inside), 3/4 inch.

Eleven pewter dispenser caps for Schroe-

der's bitters bottles have been identified in the Bertrand collection, only one of which was found in direct association with Schroeder's bottles (fig. 57).

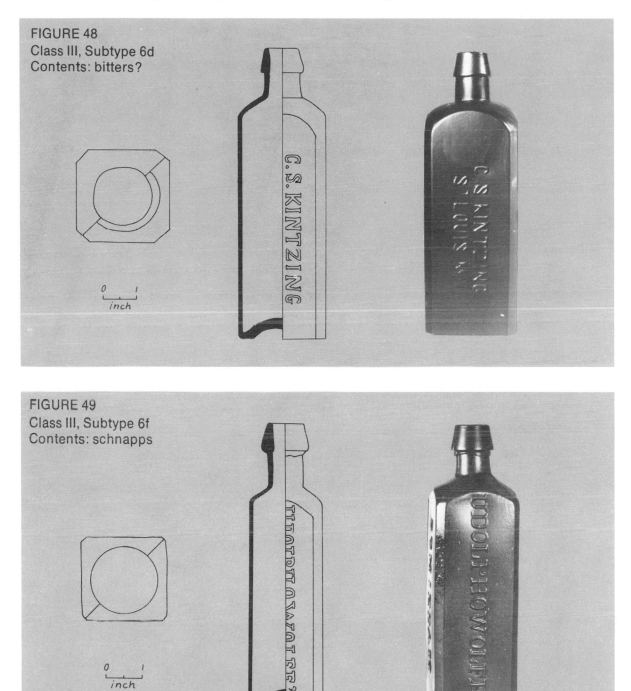

FIGURE 48
Class III, Subtype 6d
Contents: bitters?

C. S. KINTZING

0   1
inch

FIGURE 49
Class III, Subtype 6f
Contents: schnapps

UDOLPHO WOLFE'S

0   1
inch

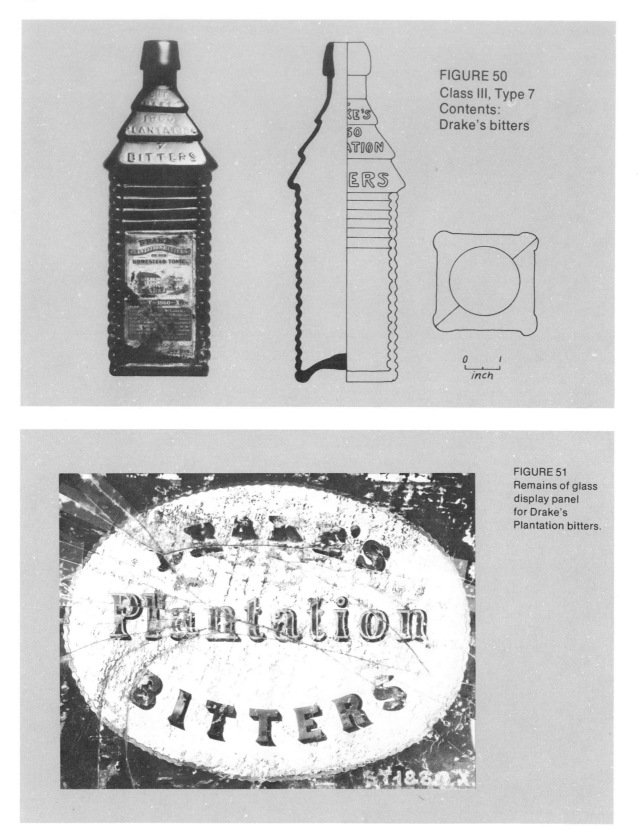

FIGURE 50
Class III, Type 7
Contents:
Drake's bitters

FIGURE 51
Remains of glass
display panel
for Drake's
Plantation bitters.

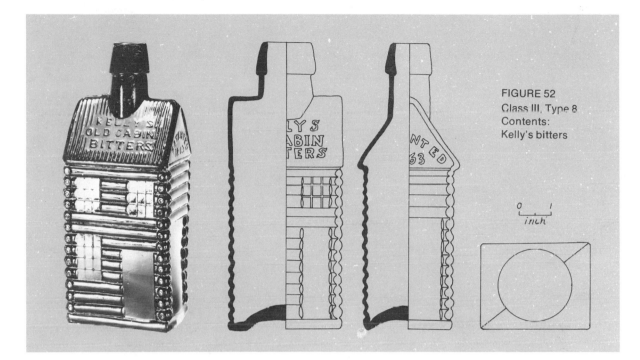

FIGURE 52
Class III, Type 8
Contents:
Kelly's bitters

FIGURE 53. Fragment of label on Kelly's Old Cabin Bitters bottle.

FIGURE 54. Artist's reconstruction of sunburst pattern on case side of Kelly's Old Cabin Bitters.

FIGURE 55. Artist's reconstruction of cabin and trees pattern on case side of Kelly's Old Cabin Bitters.

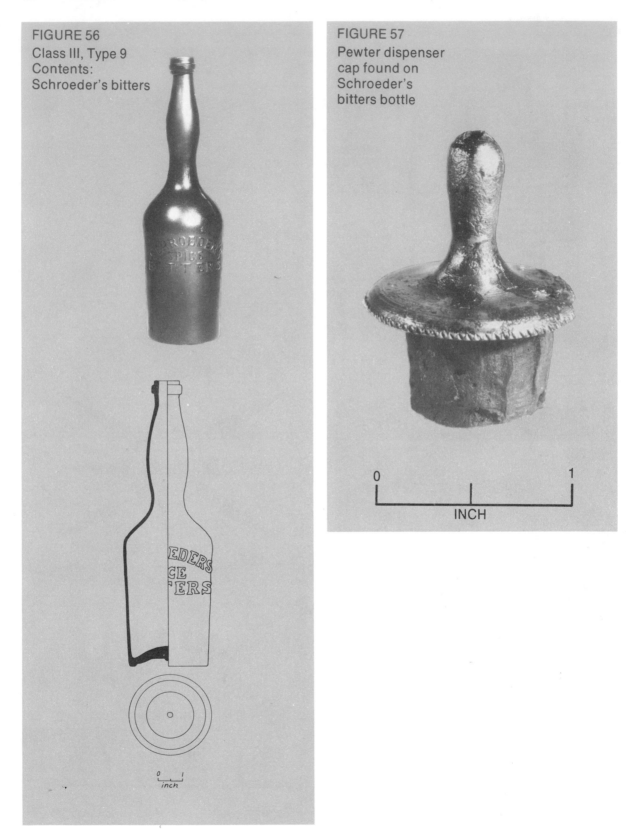

FIGURE 56
Class III, Type 9
Contents:
Schroeder's bitters

FIGURE 57
Pewter dispenser
cap found on
Schroeder's
bitters bottle

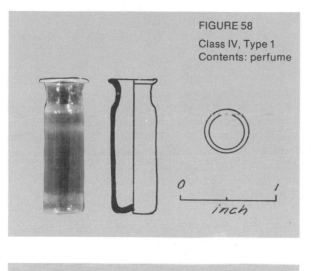

FIGURE 58

Class IV, Type 1
Contents: perfume

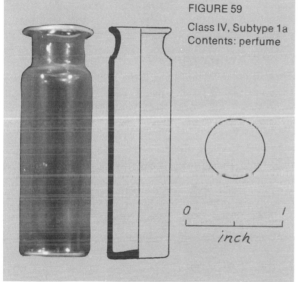

FIGURE 59

Class IV, Subtype 1a
Contents: perfume

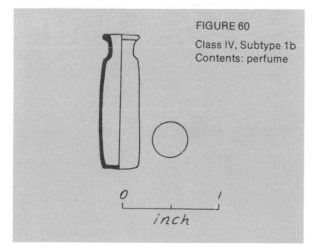

FIGURE 60

Class IV, Subtype 1b
Contents: perfume

CLASS IV
TOILETRY BOTTLES

Class IV, Type 1, Subtypes 1a, 1b:

Twenty-two small clear vials which presumably held perfume comprise Type 1 and the subtypes of Class IV (Table 8). All 22 vials were recovered from a box of personal effects labeled: "J. A. CAMPBELL." The vials have flat bases, cylindrical bodies and slightly constricted necks with flared lips. The 17 vials in Type 1 are about 1 3/8 inches in height. They are stoppered with corks, and have a capacity of .1 ounce (fig. 58). Dimensions, Type 1: height, 1 3/8 inches; diameter of base, 3/8 inch; diameter of neck (outside), 7/16 inch, (inside), 1/4 inch.

Two vials which constitute Subtype 1a are identical to those in the Type 1 description except for height (2 3/8 inches) and capacity (.3 ounce). These are pictured in Figure 59. Dimensions, Subtype 1a: height, 2 3/8 inches; diameter of base, 5/8 inch; diameter of neck (outside), 5/8 inch, (inside), 3/8 inch.

Finally, the last three vials, Subtype 1b, also match those in Type 1 morphologically, except that they are 1 3/8 inches tall and have a capacity of about .07 ounce (fig. 60). Dimensions, Subtype 1b: height, 1 3/8 inches; diameter of base, 5/16 inch; diameter of neck (outside), 3/8 inch, (inside), 1/4 inch.

CLASS V
CULINARY BOTTLES

Class V, Type 1:

At the time of this writing evidence exists for only one 12-bottle case of tall, clear, cylindrical bottles containing about one quart of whole brandied peaches (Table 9). The basal edges of these bottles are rounded and the bases exhibit high conical kick-ups (fig. 61). The bodies are cylindrical to the midpoint and taper gradually inward to wide mouths with rounded flaring lips. However, these specimens are slightly asymmetrical and vary in height and diameter, indicating that they may have been free-blown. Dimensions: height, 10 7/8 inches; diameter of base, 3 1/4 inches; diameter of neck (outside), 2 7/8 inches, (inside), 2 3/8 inches.

Each bottle is stoppered with a large cork which is covered with a thick foil seal bearing

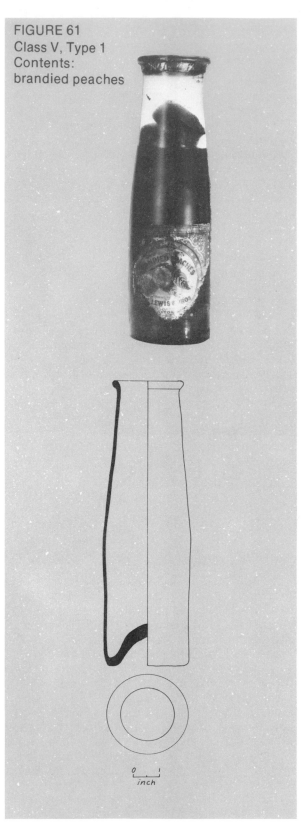

FIGURE 61
Class V, Type 1
Contents:
brandied peaches

stamped lettering at its center. The lettering reads: "W. K. LEWIS & BROTHERS / BOSTON / PRESERVES / PICKLES / SEAL'D MEATS &c." Fragments of red on white or possibly tri-colored paper labels adhere to the glass. One label was in excellent condition and is reproduced in Figure 62.

The wooden case in which the peaches were shipped was stenciled in black ink as follows: "ONE DOZEN / QUART JARS / BRANDIED PEACHES / W.K. LEWIS BROS. / BOSTON;" *consignee:* "J. MURPHY / F^t BENTON, M.T."

Class V, Type 2:

One case of 12 pale aqua-colored, transparent bottles belonging to Type 2 were recovered (Table 9). Some of these contain sliced brandied peaches, others contain brandied cherries (fig. 63). The bottles are tall and cylindrical with slightly depressed bases, each with a minute nub of glass at its center. The shoulders of these bottles, made in a three-piece mold, are rounded. The necks exhibit wide slanting collar finishes and large orifices. The bottles are stoppered with corks, but bear no label fragments. The crate in which they were packed apparently was destroyed during attempts to remove it from the cargo hold, as no records of its markings have been found. Dimensions: height 10 15/16 inches; diameter of base, 2 15/16 inches; diameter of neck (outside), 1 7/16 inches, (inside), 1 1/8 inches.

Class V, Type 3:

Laboratory records show that there are 14 whole transparent aqua glass bottles containing brandied cherries (fig. 64) and a number of bottle fragments; perhaps two cases are

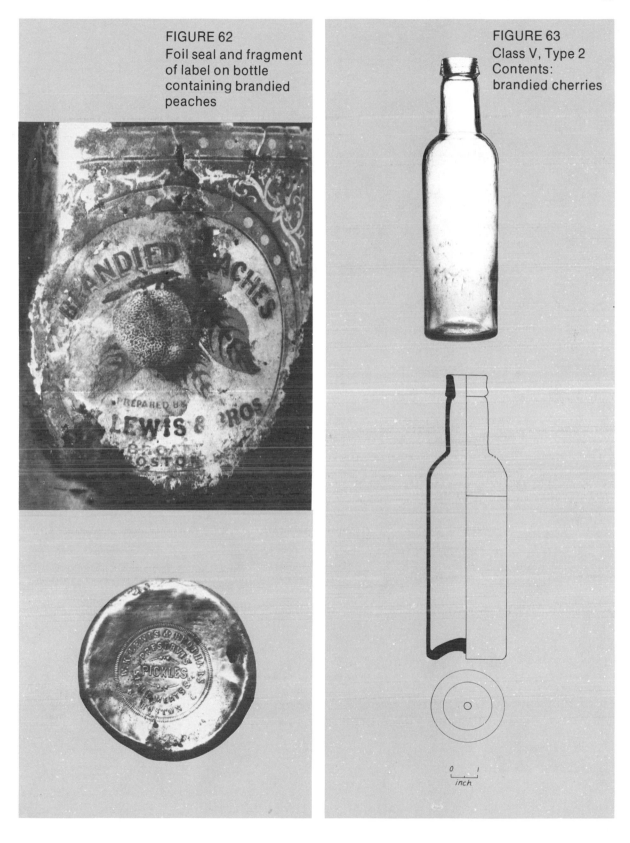

FIGURE 62
Foil seal and fragment
of label on bottle
containing brandied
peaches

FIGURE 63
Class V, Type 2
Contents:
brandied cherries

0   1
inch

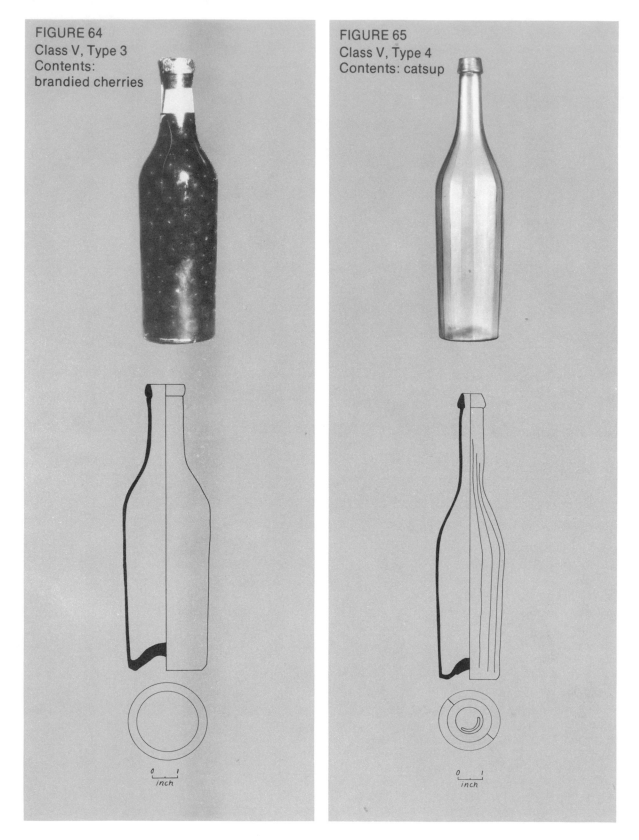

FIGURE 64
Class V, Type 3
Contents:
brandied cherries

FIGURE 65
Class V, Type 4
Contents: catsup

represented (Table 9). The basal edges of the bottles are rounded and the bases are dished. The sides expand outward from the base to the gently rounded shoulders and the necks are cylindrical, terminating in slightly rolled collars. The orifices are stoppered with corks and covered with thick plain foil seals extending a short distance onto the necks. These specimens were blown in two-piece molds and exhibit no label fragments. However, in view of the case stenciling it is not improbable that the cherries are a French product. One case in which the brandied cherries were shipped is lettered: "CERISES L'-EAU-DIE-VIE / D.S.A. / A.E."; *consignee:* "J. MURPHY / FT. BENTON." Dimensions: height, 11 1/4 inches; diameter of base, 3 inches; diameter of neck (outside), 1 9/16 inches, (inside), 1 1/4 inches.

Class V, Type 4:

Twenty-two whole bottles and a few fragments of pale aqua transparent glass constitute Type 4 (Table 9). These tall bottles containing 23 ounces of tomato catsup have slightly rounded basal edges and depressed circular bases bearing rough scars. Blown in two-piece hinged molds, the nearly cylindrical bodies exhibit 18 flat facets (fig. 65). The shoulders curve inward very gently to nearly cylindrical necks bearing applied slanted collars with flat lips. Each bottle is stoppered with a tapered cork. Hazing of the glass indicates that a large paper label once was affixed to the side of each bottle; unfortunately no labels have survived. One case is marked: " Ⓡ & CO. / UNDERWOOD & CO. / TOMATOE / KETSUP / 67 BROAD STREET / ST. LOUIS, MO." Dimensions: height, 11 15/16 inches; diameter of base, 2 9/16 inches; diameter of neck (outside), 15/16 inch, (inside), 11/16 inch.

Class V, Type 5:

Twenty whole bottles and some fragments indicate that there originally were at least two cases of 22-ounce catsup bottles of this type (Table 9). The bottles exhibit rounded basal edges and dish-shaped, depressed bottoms. The bodies expand ever so slightly from the base to the shoulder, and are marked by eight raised, flat facets separated by eight curved flutes (fig. 66). The shoulders of these

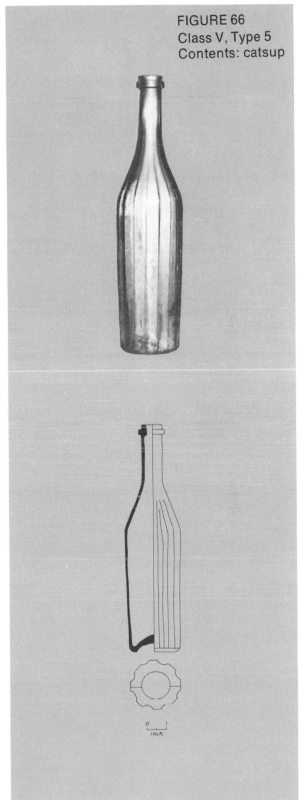

FIGURE 66
Class V, Type 5
Contents: catsup

FIGURE 67
Class V, Type 6
Contents: catsup

0   1
inch

two-piece, mold-blown bottles taper gently inward to nearly cylindrical necks bearing wine neck finishes. The whole bottles retain their original cork stoppers.

Irridescent hazing of the glass on these specimens indicates that they once bore paper labels. One case is stenciled on the end: "WM. UNDERWOOD & CO. / ST. LOUIS / N. T. CO."; "1 DOZ. / TOMATO KETCHUP / WILLIAM UNDERWOOD & CO. / 67 BROAD ST. BOSTON:; *consignee:* "J. MURPHY." Dimensions: height, 12 1/4 inches; diameter of base, est. 2 1/2 inches; diameter of neck (outside), 1 1/16 inches, (inside), 11/16 inch.

Class V, Type 6:

A total of 22 complete catsup bottles and a number of fragments are recorded in Type 6 (fig. 67). The 9 1/2-ounce bottles are aqua colored transparent glass and were blown in two-piece molds. (Table 9). The basal edges are flat, but dish-shaped circular depressions in the bases are commonly off center. The bodies are cylindrical; the shoulders are rounded but taper to nearly cylindrical necks which are finished with flat-lipped slanting collars. Dimensions: height, 8 1/2 inches; diameter of base, 2 3/8 inches; diameter of neck (outside), 7/8 inch, (inside), 5/8 inch.

Some of the bottles containing catsup are stoppered with corks. Label fragments adhering to glass read: "TOMATOE KETCHUP /_____/ TOMATO / NEW YORK." The end of one case in which the bottles were shipped is stenciled to read: "DOZ / TOMATOE KETCHUP /_____N_____." The second case bears no legible stenciling.

Class V, Type 7:

There are 45 clear glass, barrel-shaped French mustard bottles in the *Bertrand* collection and a large number of fragments (Table 9). Type 7 bottles (fig. 68) were blown in two-piece molds which represent small barrels with raised staves and bands. Bases are slightly concave and there are no shoulders or necks on the bottles. The orifices are finished with small raised bands slanting inward to the mouth. Stoppered with corks, the mouths of the bottles are covered with

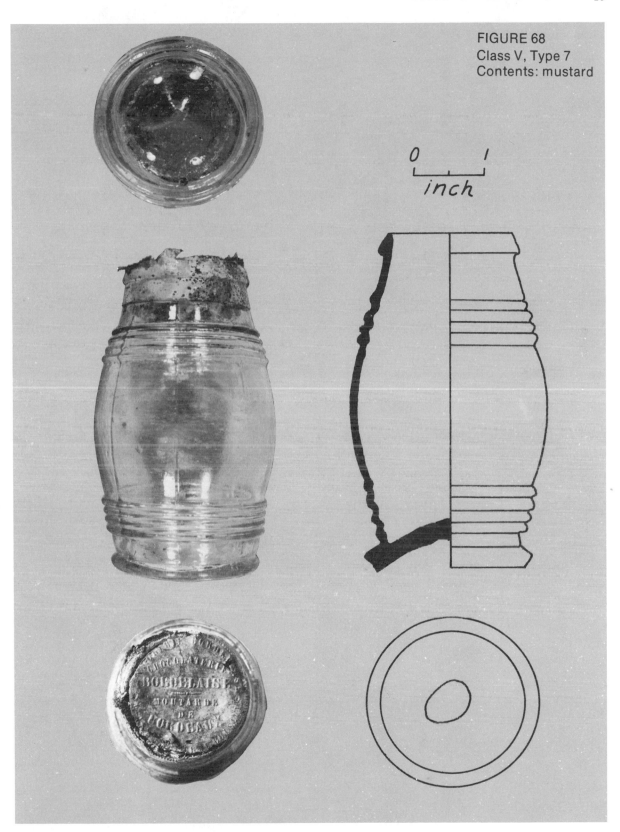

FIGURE 68
Class V, Type 7
Contents: mustard

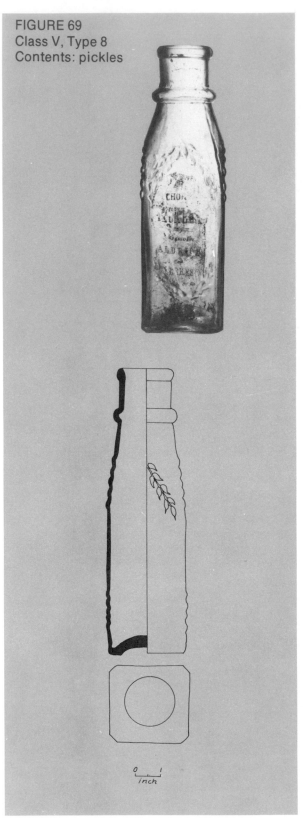

FIGURE 69
Class V, Type 8
Contents: pickles

lettered foil seals reading: "___IN ___ERLE BORDELAISE EUR AU BOUSCAT / CHOCOLATERIE BORDE-LAISE MOUTARDE DE BORDEAUX." Dimensions: height, 4 1/2 inches; diameter of base, 2 1/4 inches; diameter of neck (outside), 1 3/4 inches, (inside), 1 9/16 inches.

The squat wooden shipping cases associated with these specimens bear three kinds of black stenciled labels. The labels on the ends of the cases read as follows:

1. "STUART & CO. / DEER LODGE / MOUTARDE DE BORDEAUX / HUILE NOUVE RE_____OLTE DE 1865."
2. "WORDEN & CO. / HELL GATE / MOUTARDE DE BORDEAUX / HUILE NOUVE / RE_____OLTE DE 1865."
3. "J. MURPHY / FT. BENTON / PUR-REY & BAIRNES INC. / DE MOU-TARDE / BORDEAUX, FRANCE."

Class V, Type 8:

There are thirty 41-ounce pickle bottles and fragments in the collection (fig. 69). Half of those with their contents still intact are filled with gherkin size **pickles** and spices. The remainder of the bottles are either empty or contain mixed vegetables and spices. Made in two-piece molds, the square bodied, 11 1/4-inch tall bottles have rounded corners and gently tapered shoulders (Table 9). The edges of the bases are beveled slightly; the bases are flat except for the dished depressions at the centers. One side is framed at the top and bottom with a raised bifurcated branch or stem motif with leaves. The remaining sides bear this raised design only at the top of the side. The junction of the shoulder and neck is marked by a large bulbous ring, and the cylindrical neck is topped with a broad rounded tooled collar.

At one time each cork-stoppered bottle bore a paper label on the side, printed in **black** to read: "CHOICE / PICKLES PREPARED BY / ALDRICH / AND / YERKES / PHILA-DELPHIA." In addition the bottles had small paper labels on the necks reading: "ALD-RICH/AND/**YERKES**/PHILADELPHIA." None of the labels have survived the tests of time and water with any degree of clarity.

Another label appears on bottles containing pickled mixed vegetables and spices. The side label fragments in red letters on a blue background read: "CHOICE / MIXED / PICK-LES / C _____ S / SPICES / CANNED / FRUITS / &c. /_____/_____." The neck labels read: "PREPARED BY / ALDRICH & YERKES / PHILADEL-PHIA." Several of the bottles bearing this label exhibit remains of silver-colored foil on the collars.

The bottles were packed 12 to a case in chipped wood tow, but the field notes show no case marks for this style and size of pickle container. Dimensions: height, 11 1/4 inches; base, 3 3/16 by 3 3/16 inches; diameter of neck (outside), 2 1/8 inches, (inside), 1 13/16 inches.

Class V, Type 9, Subtypes 9a, 9b, 9c, 9d, 9e, 9f, 9g:

Type 9 is composed solely of square Gothic or cathedral style pickle jars of various sizes and styles (Table 10). Evidence exists for one 24-bottle case of 20-ounce transparent, aqua-colored jars in the Bertrand cargo. The bottles are of two types, both with the same capacity. They are 3 inches square with beveled corners and recessed Gothic panels on each side. The pyramidal shoulders slant gently to the wide, rounded rings at the bases of the cylindrical necks. The tooled, rounded ring-type collars bear straight-sided inner surfaces. The basal edges of the bottles are beveled, and the bases are flat except for the central dish-shaped depressions. Sixteen of these specimens bear two raised letters on the bases at the outer edges of the dished depressions, a "C" and an "R." The latter is upside down and back-wards. The marks could possibly be those of Curling, Ringwalt & Co., Pittsburgh, Penn-sylvania, but if so, the bottles could have been made no later than 1863 (Toulouse, 1971, p. 145). Made in two-piece molds, the bottles are stoppered with corks, but apparently none of the corks were covered with foil seals.

On 20 of the bottles the outer edges of the depressed Gothic panels bear plain columns topped with a tulip motif (fig. 70). Connecting the columns across the top of the arch is a raised inverted geometric scallop design. The topmost portions of three of the panels bear a depressed cross, at the base of which are three raised dots. The fourth panel is plain, and on some, black-and-white or red labels read:

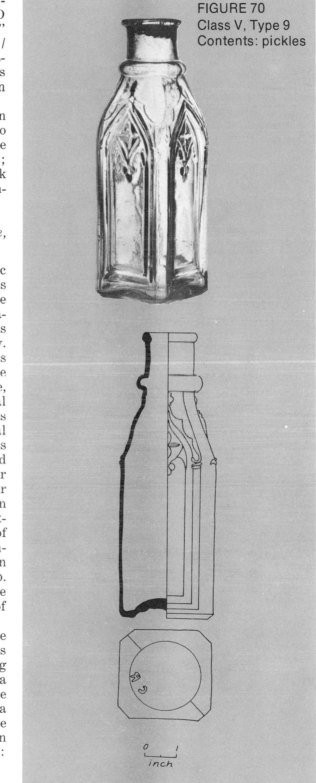

FIGURE 70
Class V, Type 9
Contents: pickles

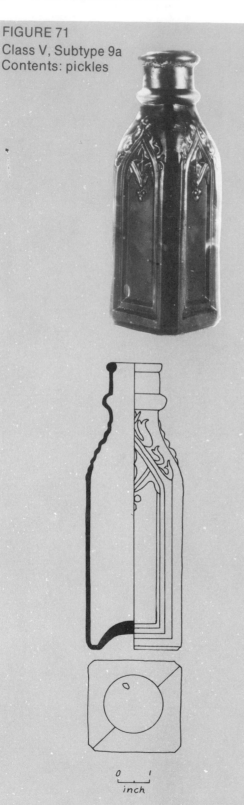

FIGURE 71
Class V, Subtype 9a
Contents: pickles

0   1
inch

"WM   U N D E R W O O D____C O.   /
_____." Some of the bottles contain
mixed vegetables, and nothing is known of the
stenciling on the associated shipping case.
Dimensions, Type 9: height, 9 5/16 inches;
base, 2 15/16 by 2 15/16 inches; diameter of
neck (outside), 1 3/4 inches, (inside), 1 3/8
inches.

The four 20-ounce Gothic pickle bottles in
Subtype 9a were packed in the same crate as
the bottles in Type 9, above. Two bottles
contain gherkin size pickles. Morphologically
these specimens are similar to those in Type 9
and differ only in the design motifs surrounding the upper parts of the Gothic panels (fig.
71). There are no columns flanking the panels,
and a raised floral motif tops the arch of each
panel. Three panels are depressed two steps
inward from the side, while the fourth panel is
plain and depressed only one step. The plain
panel once bore a tri-color label like Type 9,
fragments of which once read: "WM
U N D E R W O O D_____C O.   /
_____BROAD ST. /_____." Dimensions,
Subtype 9a: height, 9 1/8 inches; base, 2 15/16
inches; diameter of neck (outside), 1 15/16
inches, (inside), 1 5/8 inches.

In Subtype 9b there are 159 whole transparent aqua Gothic pickle jars of the 16-ounce
size, and a number of fragments (fig. 72). The
bottles are square, or nearly so, being 2 1/2
inches across each side at the base. They
stand about 8 1/2 inches tall and have rounded
corners, gently tapered pyramidal shoulders,
and double ring necks like those in Types 8
and 9. Basal edges are beveled and the flat
bases bear central dish-shaped depressions.

Three of the Gothic side panels are depressed two steps, and each panel is flanked
on either side with a column. The columns are
topped with a tulip motif and are connected
across the top of the arch by a raised inverted
scallop geometric element topped with a five-
point floral spray. At the tops of the three
panels, inset one step, are a circle with a
centrally placed cross, beneath which is a
small vertically lined element, and another
spray-like motif. The second inset step of each
of the three panels forms a small arched panel
within the larger one. The fourth panel is
completely plain and is inset only one step
from the face of the side. Presumably the
fourth panel at one time bore a paper label.
Dimensions, Subtype 9b: height, 8 9/16 inch-

es; base, 2 5/8 by 2 5/8 inches; diameter of neck (outside), 1 15/16 inches, (inside), 1 3/8 inches.

The bottles, many of which contain mixed vegetables, peppers, plum tomatoes, or small gherkins with spices, are stoppered with corks. The corks on some bottles are covered with coal tar, over which plain foil seals have been crimped. Packed in one dozen lots in chipped wood tow, the wooden boxes are labeled in a variety of ways as follows:

1. "S. ROUCH CO. / WHOLESALER"; "GERKINS / GITHENS, REXAMER & CO. / OFFICE 104/ DELAWARE MARKET"; *consignee:* "VIVIAN AND SIMPSON / VIRGINIA CITY, M.T."
2. "GERKINS / GITHENS, REXAMER & CO. / DELAWARE MARKET / DELAWARE RIVER PICKLE & / PRESERVE WORKS"; *consignee:* "J. MURPHY / FT. BENTON, MT."
3. "1 DOZ. QTS. ASSORTED PICKLES / DELAWARE RIVER PICKLE & / PRESERVE WORKS / GITHENS, REXAMER & CO. / OFFICE 104 / DELAWARE MARKET"; "RAIL & RIVER / S. R. & CO. / ST. LOUIS, MO."; *consignee:* "VIVIAN AND SIMPSON."

There are 10 whole, 14-ounce bottles in Subtype 9c, and a number of fragments composing two more bottles. The bottles are like Subtype 9a bottles, but are of a smaller capacity (fig. 73). Corks and seals are the same as in Subtype 9c, and the consignee was Worden and Company in Hell Gate. Evidence for only one case of these bottles appears in the collection records. Dimensions, Subtype 9c: height, 7 3/16 inches; base, 2 1/2 by 2 1/2 inches; diameter of neck (outside), 1 1/2 inches, (inside), 1 1/8 inches.

One group of twenty-four, 14-ounce cathedral pickle bottles compose Subtype 9d (fig. 74). These bottles are like those in Type 9 and Subtype 9e except in capacity, the absence of a plain label panel, and a variation in the raised design elements capping the panels. The spray-like element capping three of the panels of each bottle has five rays, and the fourth panel has a three-ray element. Nothing is known concerning the markings on the case in which they were shipped. Dimensions, Sub-

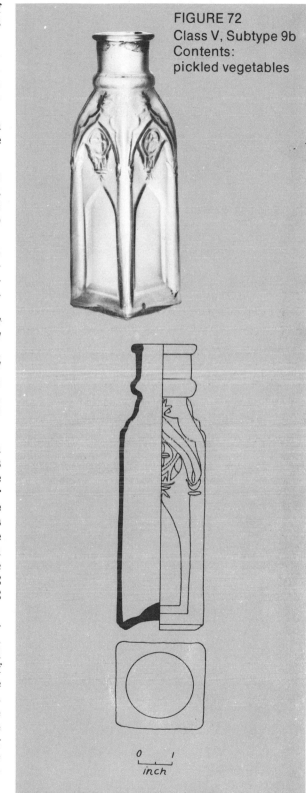

FIGURE 72
Class V, Subtype 9b
Contents:
pickled vegetables

0   1
inch

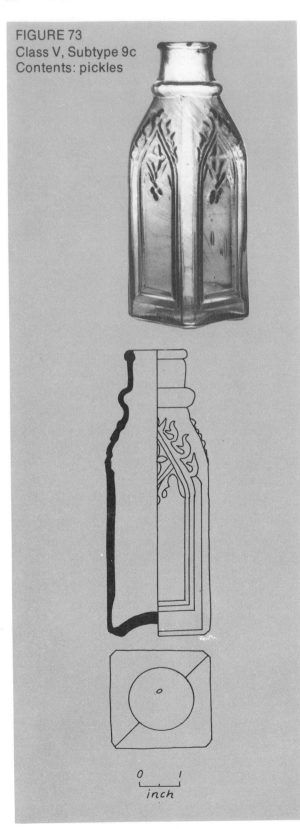

FIGURE 73
Class V, Subtype 9c
Contents: pickles

0   1
inch

type 9d: height, 7 1/2 inches; base, 2 3/8 by 2 3/8 inches; diameter of neck (outside), 1 11/16 inches, (inside), 1 3/8 inches.

There are nine 24-bottle cases of whole or fragmentary 10-ounce Gothic pickle bottles in Subtype 9e which contain white clover honey from Philadelphia (fig. 75). They are small in capacity and lack columns which flank the side panels on some other types. The uppermost of the depressed, arch-shaped panels bear raised cross hatchure and three horizontal bars at the lower extremities. The 7 5/16-inch tall bottles are stoppered with corks and coal tar covered with foil seals, none of which remain intact. Dimensions, Subtype 9e: height, 7 5/16 inches; base, 2 1/4 by 2 1/4 inches; diameter of neck (outside), 1 5/16 inches, (inside), 1 1/16 inches.

Black and white paper labels affixed to plain side panels of individual bottles are fragmentary, but read: "W_____/ CLOVER / HONEY /_____/ ALDRICH / & / YERKES / N_____/_____." The black stenciling on the wooden cases reads: "2 DOZ. NET / WHITE CLOVER HONEY / FROM / ALDRICH & YERKES, PHILADELPHIA;" *consignee:* "VIVIAN & SIMPSON / VIRGINIA CITY, M.T."

Subtype 9f bottles, containing approximately 10 ounces of honey are also of the Gothic style (fig. 76). Blown in two-piece molds, these 7 1/4-inch tall bottles are square, with beveled corners and gently slanted pyramidal shoulders. The basal edges are beveled and the bases are flat except for the central dish-shaped depressions. They exhibit a wide convex ring at the base of the neck and a tooled ring collar at the orifice. Three of the sides on each bottle bear Gothic panels of two sizes set one above the other, both of which are depressed two steps from the face of the side. The point of the arch on the uppermost panel bears a raised three-element spray motif. The centers of both arches are filled with a raised diamond cross-hatchured motif. On the fourth side, the lower panel is plain and once held a paper label.

A thick foil seal lettered "W. K. LEWIS & BROTHERS   /   PRESERVES /... ▄▄◗◖▄▄   ... /   PICKLES /... ▄▄◗◖▄▄ ... / SEAL'D MEATS &c. / BOSTON" covers the coal-tar-covered cork stopper. The lids to the wooden cases, and the end pieces were lettered in black ink to read:

"TWO DOZEN PINTS / HONEY / FROM / W. K. LEWIS & BROTHERS, BOSTON"; *consignee:* "STUART & Cº. / DEER LODGE, M.T."; "1 DOZEN PINTS / HONEY / FROM / W. K. LEWIS & BROTHER, BOSTON"; *consignee:* "WORDEN & CO. / HELL GATE, M.T." There are 50 whole bottles and many fragments of this subtype in the collection. Dimensions, Subtype 9f: height, 7 1/16 inches; base, 2 1/4 by 2 1/4 inches; diameter of neck, (outside), 1 5/8 inches, (inside), 1 3/16 inches.

Subtype 9g (fig. 77) consists of one case of 12 bottles containing tamarind fruit found in the *Bertrand* cargo. These 10-ounce Gothic pickle bottles are quite similar, except in capacity, the lack of columns flanking the cathedral panels, and a cross motif at the top of the arch, to Type 9 bottles. The bottles which still retain their contents are stoppered with corks and coal tar, covered with lettered foil seals reading " W. K. LEWIS & BROTHERS / PRESERVES /...➤•◄.../ PICKLES /... ➤•◄ ... / SEAL'D MEATS &c. / BOSTON." The bottled tamarinds were packed in a wooden case marked: "ONE DOZEN PINTS / TAMARINDS / FROM / W. K. LEWIS & BROS., BOSTON"; *consignee:* TO: WORDEN & CO., HELL GATE." Dimensions, Subtype 9g: height, 7 3/16 inches; base, 2 1/4 by 2 1/4 inches; diameter of neck, (outside), 1 7/16 inches, (inside), 1 1/8 inches.

Class V., Type 10, Subtype 10a:

Shipped in one dozen bottle lots, the 173 square Gothic letter-paneled pepper sauce bottles in Type 10 are most interesting (Table 11). Made of transparent pale greenish glass, these 5-ounce bottles stand 8 3/4 inches to 8 7/8 inches high and are square bodied with rounded corners. The base of each bottle is flat and bears a central dish-shaped depression. Basal edges are beveled. Each of the four sides of the bottle bears a Gothic window-shaped panel inset from the face of the side and framed with another small ridge of glass. Above each arch on the pyramidal shoulders of the bottle are inset frames filled with raised diamond or lattice cross-hatchure. The necks are long and cylindrical and terminate in smooth rounded tooled collars composed of two rings, the lowermost of which is beveled. The closures in all cases are corks. Dimen-

FIGURE 74
Class V, Subtype 9d
Contents: pickles

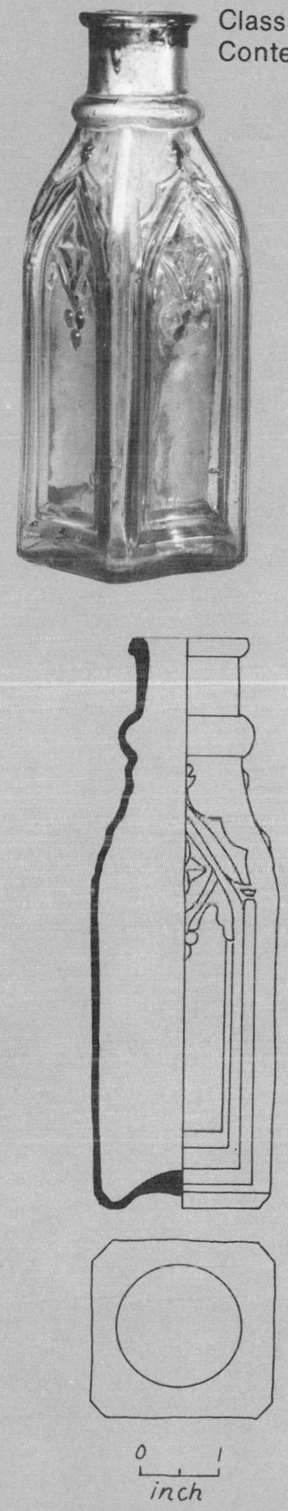

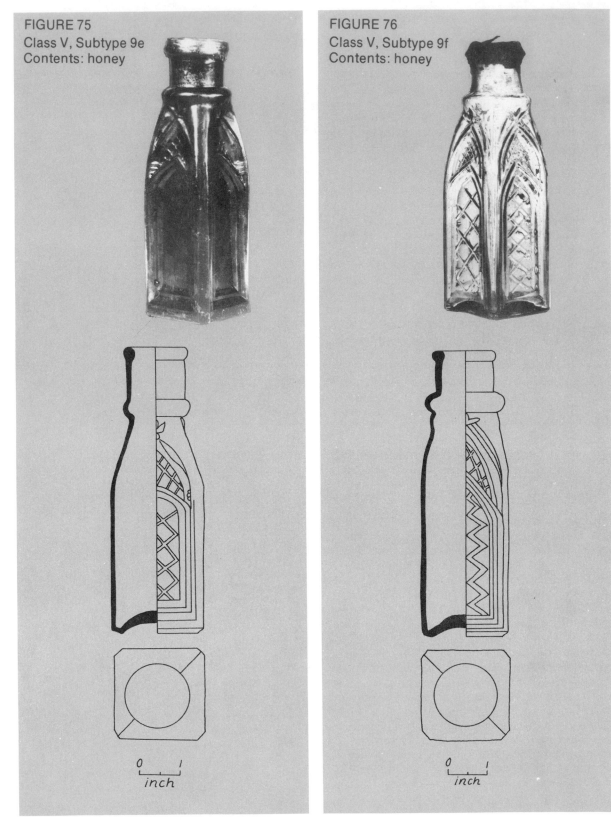

FIGURE 75
Class V, Subtype 9e
Contents: honey

FIGURE 76
Class V, Subtype 9f
Contents: honey

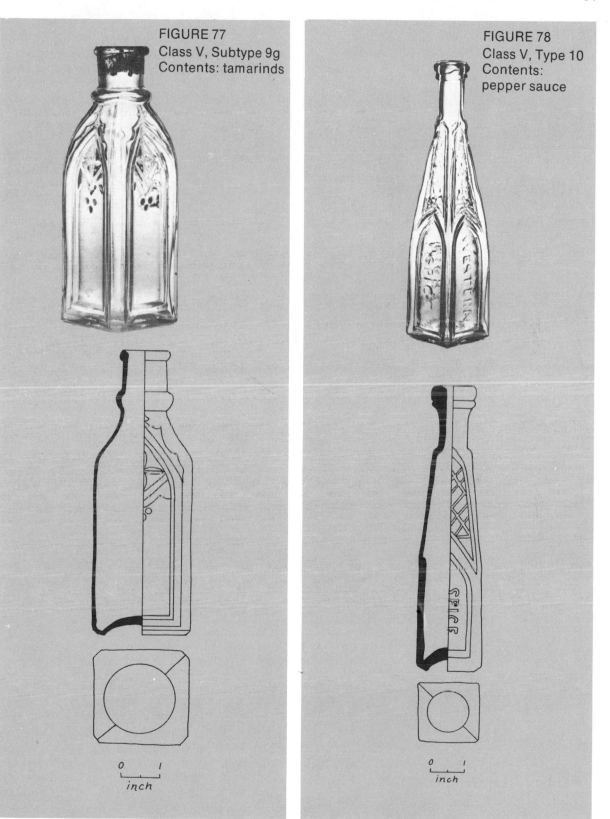

FIGURE 77
Class V, Subtype 9g
Contents: tamarinds

FIGURE 78
Class V, Type 10
Contents:
pepper sauce

0   1
inch

0   1
inch

FIGURE 79
Class V, Subtype 10a
Contents: pepper sauce

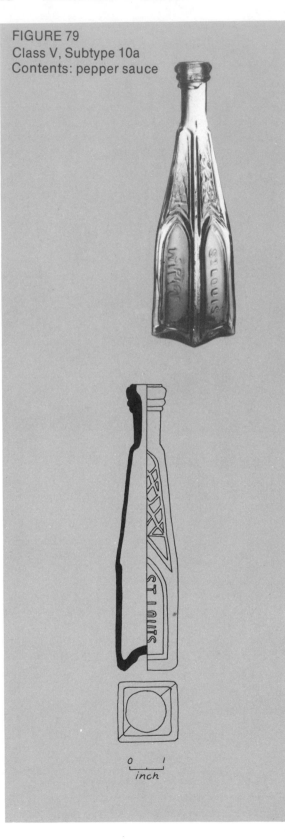

sions, Type 10: height, 8 5/8 inches; base, 1 7/8 by 1 7/8 inches; diameter of neck, (outside), 1 1/8 inches; (inside), 11/16 inch.

Perhaps the most striking feature of these particular bottles, and those in Subtype 10a, is the raised lettering which appears in a vertical line on each of three side panels. Type 10 specimens (fig. 78) are lettered "WESTERN / SPICE / MILLS"; the fourth panel is plain and probably once bore a paper label. Thirty-six of these bottles containing catsup were packed in cases marked as follows:

1. "_____OTHIC /_____B_____";
   "THIS SIDE UP WITH CARE";
   "WESTERN /_____E MILLS / TO-
   MATO / CATSUP / ST. LOUIS, MO. /
   ---⋅--- / ONE DOZEN."
2. "ONE DOZEN / WESTERN / SPICE
   MILLS / TOMATOE / CATSUP / ST.
   LOUIS, MO"; "GLASS / THIS SIDE
   UP WITH CARE / GOTHIC /
   _____ / Ft. BENTON."

The 79 bottles in Subtype 10a are morphologically like those in Type 10 except that the panel lettering reads "ST LOUIS / SPICE / MILLS" (fig. 79). Both kinds of bottles were found in 18 individual crates marked:

1. "WARRANTED EXTRA / PEPPER
   SAUCE / FOR FAMILY USE" (fig.
   80); "_____ / Ft. BENTON."
2. "WARRANTED EXTRA / PEPPER
   SAUCE / FOR FAMILY USE";
   "   / FT BENTON / THIS
   SIDE UP WITH CARE."

Dimensions, Subtype 10a: height, 8 5/8 inches; base, 1 1/8 by 1 1/8 inches; diameter of neck, (outside), 1 1/16 inches, (inside), 3/4 inch.

Class V, Type 11:

Shipped in case lots of 24 bottles, there are 95 whole bottles and one broken specimen in Type 11 (Table 11). They are cathedral paneled pepper sauce bottles with hexagonal bodies and shoulders, rounded corners, and tall cylindrical necks (fig. 81). The body of each 6 1/2-ounce bottle bears six inset Gothic panels or windows, two opposing pairs of which have an extra ridge of glass forming a frame around the circumference. Above each panel on the shoulders are smaller five-sided windows with a central depressed three-lobed element. A single floral motif tops each small window on the shoulders. The necks terminate in relatively wide rounded tooled collars with slightly beveled rims at the bases. The bases of the bottles are slightly dished. Dimensions: height, 8 3/4 inches; diameter of base, 1 3/16 inches; diameter of neck, (outside), 1 3/16 inches, (inside), 3/4 inch.

Shipping cases for the pepper sauce bottles were labeled as follows:

1. "SUPERIOR / RED BIRD / PEPPER / SAUCE / NEW YORK"; *consignee:* "TO: J. MURPHY / Ft. BENTON / VIA C.S.K., ST. LOUIS, MO."
2. "B_____ / PEPPER / SAUCE / NEW YORK"; *consignee:* "STUART & CO. / DEER LODGE."
3. "SUPERIOR / BIRD / PEPPER / SAUCE / NEW YORK"; *consignee:* "J. MURPHY/ FT. BENTON, M.T. / VIA C. S. K. / ST. LOUIS, MO."

Class V, Type 12:

Thirty-three bottles and a few fragments comprise Type 12 (Table 11). The transparent pale aqua-colored club sauce bottles have cylindrical bodies lettered vertically on one side to read "E. F. DIXIE" (fig. 82). The bases exhibit moderately deep dished depressions and rough scars. The rounded shoulders of these 12 1/3-ounce bottles are lettered horizontally on one side to read "WORCESTER," and on the other side "SAUCE." Made in two-piece molds, they are 8 1/2 inches tall and are finished with a triple ring collar bearing a flat lip. The mouth and that part of the neck interior enclosed or covered by the collar is funnel-shaped to accomodate a lettered glass stopper. Dimensions: height, 8 1/2 inches; diameter of base, 2 9/16 inches; diameter of neck (outside), 1 inch, (inside), 5/8 inch.

The club sauce stoppers are flat on top, with beveled edges and straight sides. Raised lettering on the tops of the stoppers reads: "LEA & PERRINS." The tapered stems are not ground, and bear the marks of what probably were three-piece molds. The stems are sleeved in cork.

Field information indicates that the three dozen bottles of sauce were shipped from New York, and were on their way to Stuart and Co. in Deer Lodge, Montana Territory.

FIGURE 80. *Artist's reconstruction of stenciling on case of pepper sauce from the St. Louis Spice Mills.*

Class V, Type 13:

Evidence exists for eight dozen 6-ounce London Club Sauce bottles (Table 11). There are 76 whole bottles and many fragments in the collection. Made in two-piece molds with pale aqua transparent glass, these small bottles have cylindrical bodies, very slightly dished bases, long tapering necks and rounded shoulders. The molds in which the bottles were blown may have been chilled iron, inasmuch as the bottles look like hammered metal in reflected light. The neck finish is composed of a rounded, tooled, ring-type collar with a flared extension at its base. One side of the body is lettered vertically "PARKER BROS." (fig. 83). The shoulders bear raised letters reading "LONDON CLUB SAUCE." Most of the whole bottles still contain the dark brown sauce, and are stoppered with corks. Dimensions: height, 7 1/8 inches; diameter of base, 2 inches; diameter of neck, (outside), 1 3/8 inches, (inside), 9/16 inch.

The wooden shipping cases which held the bottles are wood burned to read: "LONDON CLUB SAUCE / A.J. PARKER / N.Y. / SOLE AGENT FOR THE / U.S." (fig. 84); "2 DOZ. / PARKER BROS. / LONDON CLUB

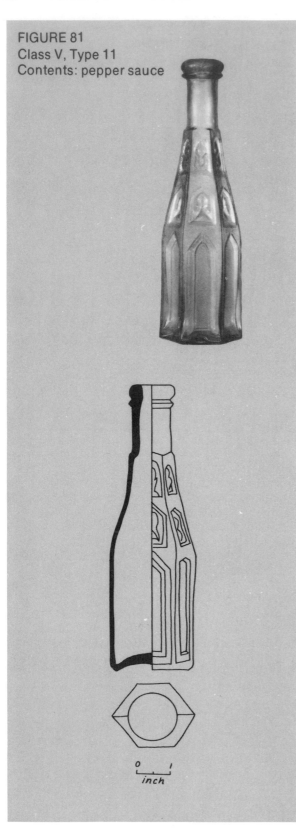

FIGURE 81
Class V, Type 11
Contents: pepper sauce

0   1
inch

SAUCE / J. PARKER / N.Y. / AGENT FOR THE / U.S."; "ST. LOUIS, MO. / SPAULD-INGS /_____/ EXPRESS / PML M_____C / _____ B _____O _____."

Class V, Type 14:

Two 12-bottle cases of lemon syrup were recovered from the *Bertrand,* of which 23 bottles have survived intact (Table 11). The 16-ounce containers are tall and cylindrical with long tapered necks and slanted collar neck finishes (fig. 85). The dished basal depressions are inset one step or ring from the flat edges of the bases. The centers of the basal depressions bear small nubs. The transparent, pale aqua-colored, bubbly glass bottles stand 10 1/4 inches tall and were blown in three-piece molds. All of the bottles have (or have had) cork stoppers. Dimensions: height, 10 1/4 inches; diameter of base, 2 9/16 inches; diameter of neck, (outside), 15/16 inch, (inside), 3/4 inch.

Stenciling on the wooden cases reads: "LEMON / SYRUP / MANUFACTURED BY / MEYER & MINISTER / ST. LOUIS, MO."; "BAR STORES / BERTRAND"; "1 DOZ. LEMON SYRUP /_____/ WHOLESALE CONFECTIONER / 74 THIRD ST. / ST. LOUIS."

Class V, Type 15:

Bottles containing ground black pepper comprise Type 15 (Table 12). Morphologically, according to an 1880 bottle catalogue, *Whitall, Tatum & Co.* (1971, p. 49), these 26 bottles are of the mustard or horseradish shape. They are rather tall (6 3/4 inches) with eight sides, sloping shoulders, and slightly tapered necks finished with asymmetrical rolled collars. They were blown in two-piece molds in transparent pale greenish-aqua colored bubbly glass. The bases are flat and the sides are fluted or slightly depressed. These cork-stoppered bottles hold about 8 1/4 ounces and are 1 inch in diameter at the mouth (fig. 86). A black-on-white paper cap was once affixed over the cork, but apparently the cap was not lettered. Dimensions: height, 6 3/4 inches; base, 1 5/8 by 5/8 by 15/16 inches; diameter of neck (outside), 1 1/4 inches, (inside), 1 inch.

Presumably all of these bottles originally bore black-on-white paper labels with print on both sides. Fragments which have been pieced together show the front side of the label with a plain three-line border and print reading "NU__M____/ XXX /_____ACK PEP-PER," beneath which is pictured an eagle clutching a banner reading "E PLUR BUS UN____." Beneath the eagle is a union style, vertically striped shield with olive branches protruding from the right side and arrows protruding from the left. Print beneath the eagle and shield is illegible. Print on the backs of the labels runs vertically and reads: "_____ of the tub and character of the water; a tabl_____/_____of water. For all other purposes for which POI_____/ _____N_____OS SELECT SPICES / nrod, (Lined with Paper,) and full Wier_____/_____E PEPPER; _____LEN____CE, _____E /_____CINNAMON, MACE /_____this with confidence."

Field notes do not indicate the number of bottles contained in a single case, but black stenciled case labeling on one case reads: "ALLEN MILLS / BLACK PEPPER / NEW YORK / B. S. GRANT & CO. / WHOLESALE / GROCER / NO. 5317_____/ ST. LOUIS, MO."; "B. S. GRANT & CO."

Class V, Type 16:

Sixty-five bottles containing horseradish and many glass fragments indicate that there may have been three 2-dozen bottle lots in Type 16 (Table 12). Blown in two-piece molds, the bottles have cylindrical bodies and short cylindrical necks with sharp edged "blow over" finishes and cork stoppers (fig. 87). Near the base, adjacent to the mold mark on one side is a small irregular raised mark. The bases of these 7-ounce transparent aqua-colored bottles are flat. Dimensions : height, 4 7/8 inches; diameter of base, 2 1/8 inches; diameter of neck, (outside), 1 5/16 inches, (inside), 1 1/8 inches.

The assorted shipping cases are stenciled: "2 DOZ. / HORSE_____"; "_____/ HORSERADISH /_____/ 2603 SIXTH STREET / CIN., O."

Class V, Type 17:

All of the 38 whole free-blown olive oil bottles in Type 17 are asymmetrical and have deep conical kick-ups lacking pontil scars (Table 12). Stoppered with foil-covered corks, these 9 1/4-inch, 8 1/2-ounce, nearly cylindri-

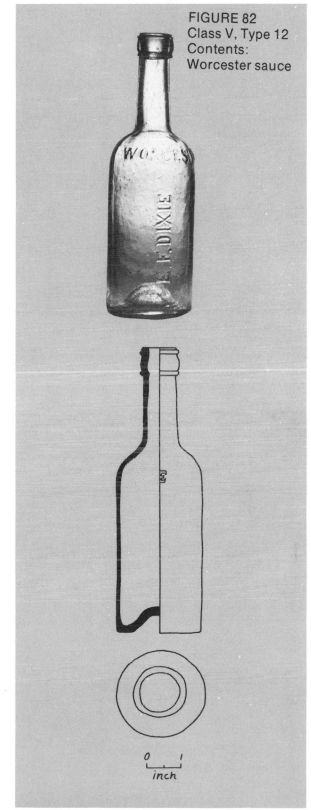

FIGURE 82
Class V, Type 12
Contents:
Worcester sauce

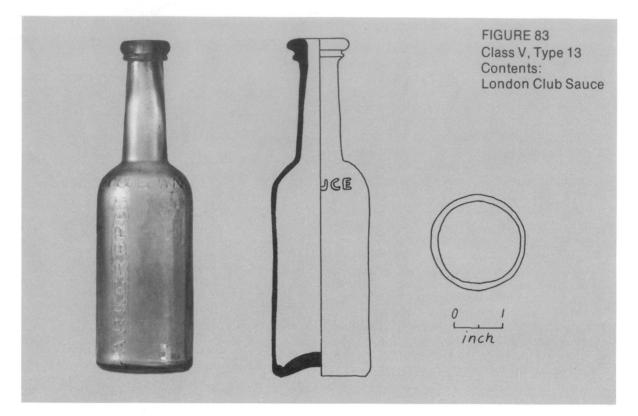

FIGURE 83
Class V, Type 13
Contents:
London Club Sauce

FIGURE 84

Side of case containing
bottles of London Club Sauce

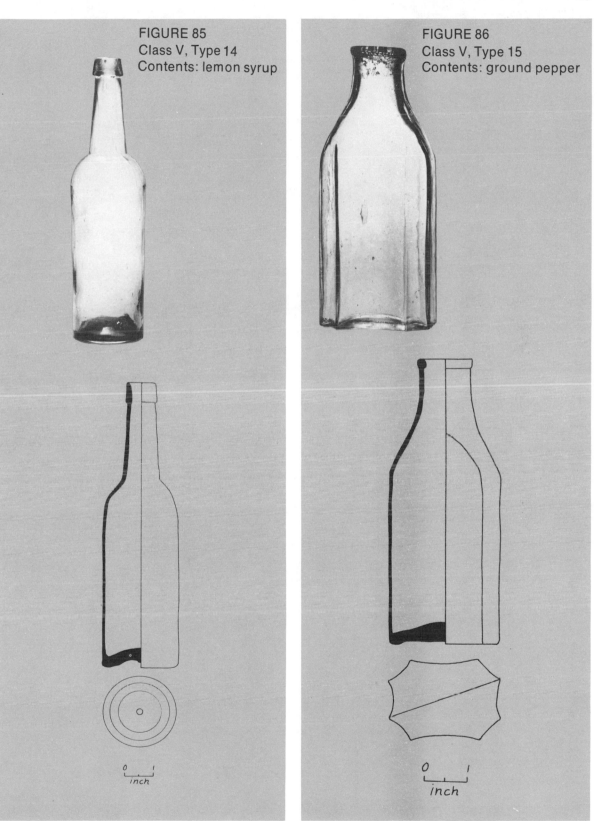

FIGURE 85
Class V, Type 14
Contents: lemon syrup

FIGURE 86
Class V, Type 15
Contents: ground pepper

0   1
inch

0   1
inch

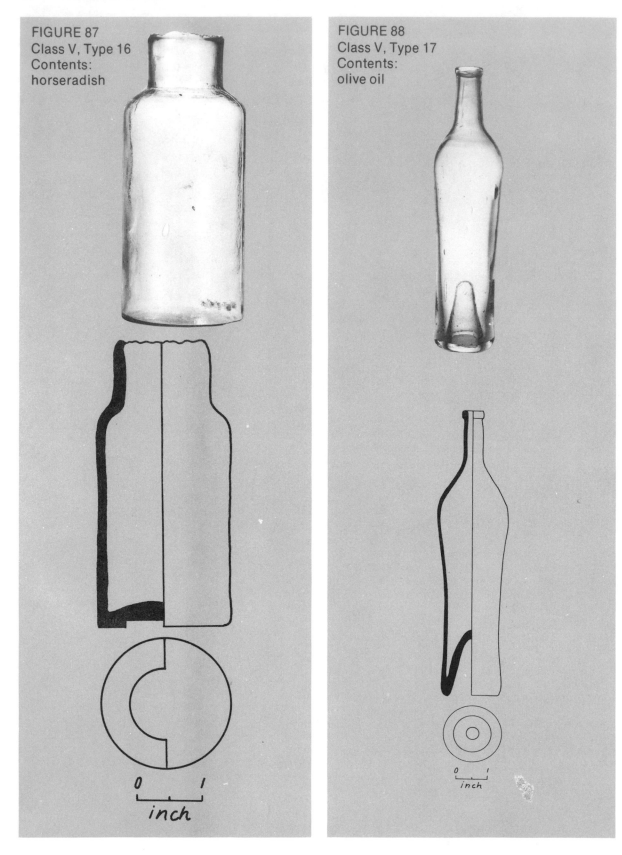

FIGURE 87
Class V, Type 16
Contents:
horseradish

FIGURE 88
Class V, Type 17
Contents:
olive oil

cal bodied bottles are smaller in diameter at the bases than at the shoulders (fig. 88). The shoulders slope gently upward to the nearly cylindrical necks which terminate in smooth flat-lipped collars just slightly larger in diameter than the necks. Dimensions: height, 9 1/4 inches; diameter of base, 1 15/16 inches; diameter of neck, (outside), 7/8 inch, (inside), 5/8 inch.

Whole bottles and fragments indicate there were at least two cases of imported French olive oil. One case, according to field notes, is marked: "POSSELFIT / HUILE / D'OLIVE / SURFINE / MARSEILLE"; *consignee:* *"WORDEN & CO., HELL GATE."*

Class V, Type 18:

Blown in two-piece molds and finished with a patent lip at the neck terminus, collection information indicates there are at least 131 1/2-ounce lemon oil vials and some fragments in the cargo (Table 12). These tiny bottles have flat bases, cylindrical bodies, conical shoulders and cylindrical necks (fig. 89). They are made of transparent, nearly colorless glass and many are stoppered with corks. Dimensions: height, 2 1/8 inches; diameter of base, 7/8 inch; diameter of neck, (outside), 5/8 inch, (inside), 3/8 inch.

One of these small 2-inch vials was packed inside a can of "Sugar of Lemons," a powdered form of lemonade. The contents of one can, when mixed with water, made about five quarts of lemonade. Although the labels on the tops of the cans do not contribute to the morphology of the glass vials, they are historically interesting and are shown in Figure 90. "Sugar of Lemons" were packed 24 cans per wooden case, but other field information is lacking.

Class V, Type 19:

At least four 24-bottle cases of assorted jellies and 32 additional bottles about which there is no information have been recorded in the cargo of the *Bertrand* (Table 12). These 5-inch, 1/2-pint, wide mouth bottles display cylindrical bodies, slightly flared necks and thin rolled collars (fig. 91). The bases are dished and exhibit pontil scars. Dimensions: height, 5 inches; diameter of base, 1 13/16 inches; diameter of neck, (outside), 1 1/2 inches, (inside), 1 1/4 inches.

The bottles from at least four cases contained several kinds of jellies, including cur-

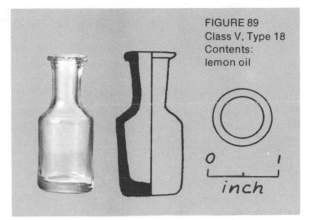

FIGURE 89
Class V, Type 18
Contents:
lemon oil

rant, apple, strawberry, raspberry, and quince. Stoppered with corks covered by thin foil wrappers extending onto the necks, the bottles display four-color paper labels with an eagle in the center. The variety of jelly contained in a jar was identified on the label, followed by: "PREPARED BY / NUMSEN, CARROLL & Co / BALTIMORE," in red ink. (fig. 92). The cases in which the jellies were shipped are marked in black "2 DOZ 1/2 PINTS / ASSORTED / JELLY"; *consignee:* "VIVIAN & SIMPSON / VIRGINIA CITY, M.T. / ST. LOUIS."

The second group of 32 bottles and fragments differ only in the label fragments. Apparently, one label was red and black on white, but the text is not discernable.

FIGURE 90. Paper label affixed to can containing lemon oil, for the preparation of lemonade.

FIGURE 91

Class V, Type 19
Contents:
assorted jellies

0   1
inch

FIGURE 92. Artist's reconstruction of label on
jelly jar (fig. 91).

CLASS VI
INK CONTAINERS

Class VI, Type 1:

Ninety-two whole bottles and fragments of six others from one complete case of four dozen small, octagonal, transparent, aqua-colored ink bottles and most of a second case were taken from the steamer *Bertrand* (Table 13). All of these 1 1/2-ounce bottles or ink wells are mold blown and exhibit plain flat bases (fig. 93). The eight side panels are three-quarters of an inch wide and end in slightly curved arcs at the shoulders. The slightly rounded shoulders are nearly perpendicular to the sides; the necks are short and nearly cylindrical. The 7/8-inch-diameter collars are squared, with flat lips at the mouths in patent lip style. The orifices measure 9/16 inch in diameter. The bottles vary in height from 2 1/4 inches to 2 1/2 inches; some contain red or brown ink, but the majority contain a blue-black liquid. Dimensions: height, 2 3/8 inches; diameter of base, 1 13/16 inches; diameter of neck, (outside), 7/8 inch, (inside), 1/2 inch.

The cases were marked in black stencil ink as follows: "4 DOZ. INK / R. B. SNOW / ST. LOUIS, MO."; "15 LBS."; *consignee:* "G. P. DORRIS / VIRGINIA CITY / MONTANA TE."

Class VI, Type 2:

One case of 24 cylindrical, wheel-thrown stoneware ink bottles constitute Type 2 (Table 13). The brown salt glazed bottles have flat unglazed bases, slightly concave conical shoulders and relatively wide flaring collars with flat lips (fig. 94). Each bottle is impressed on the side, near the base: "VITREOUS STONE BOTTLES / J. BOURNE & SON, / PATENTEES / DENBY & CODNER PARK POTTERIES / NEAR DERBY. / P. & J. ARNOLD/ LONDON." Dimensions: height, 7 inches; diameter of base, 3 inches; diameter of neck, (outside), 1 13/16 inches, (inside), 1 inch.

The bottles, containing about 14 ounces of green ink, vary in height from 7 1/8 to 7 1/2 inches. They are stoppered with corks, and sealed with a gray putty-like material stamped "ARNOLD / LONDON." According to Wilson (1974 In Press) the bottles originally had paper labels. A few black-on-red label fragments with cross-hatched borders were found on the Bertrand bottles.

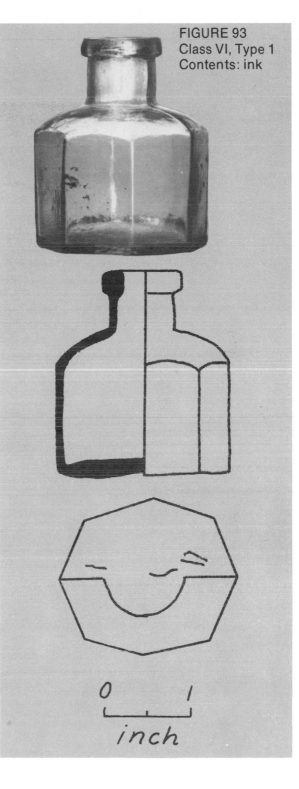

FIGURE 93
Class VI, Type 1
Contents: ink

0   1

inch

The wooden case in which they were shipped is stenciled: "ARNOLDS INKS / OIL / VIVIAN & SIMPSON."

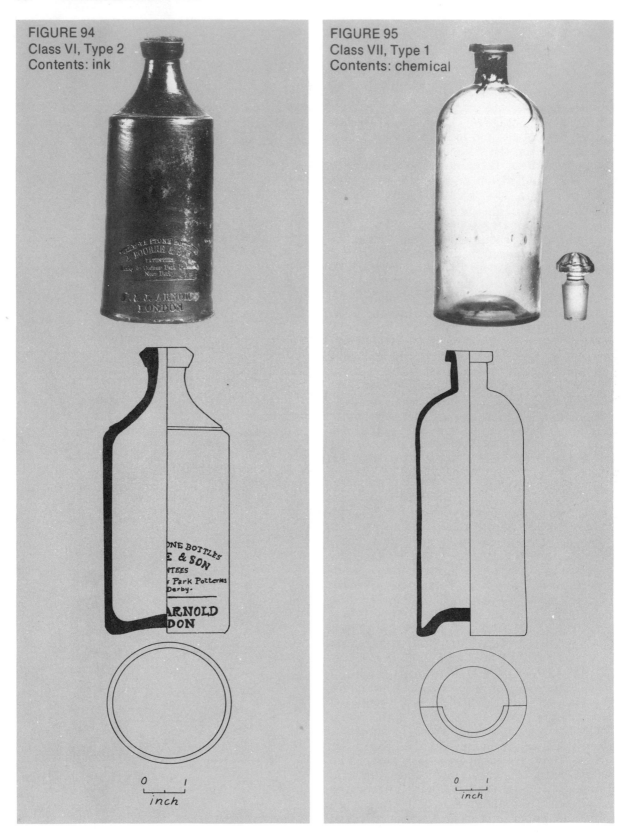

FIGURE 94
Class VI, Type 2
Contents: ink

FIGURE 95
Class VII, Type 1
Contents: chemical

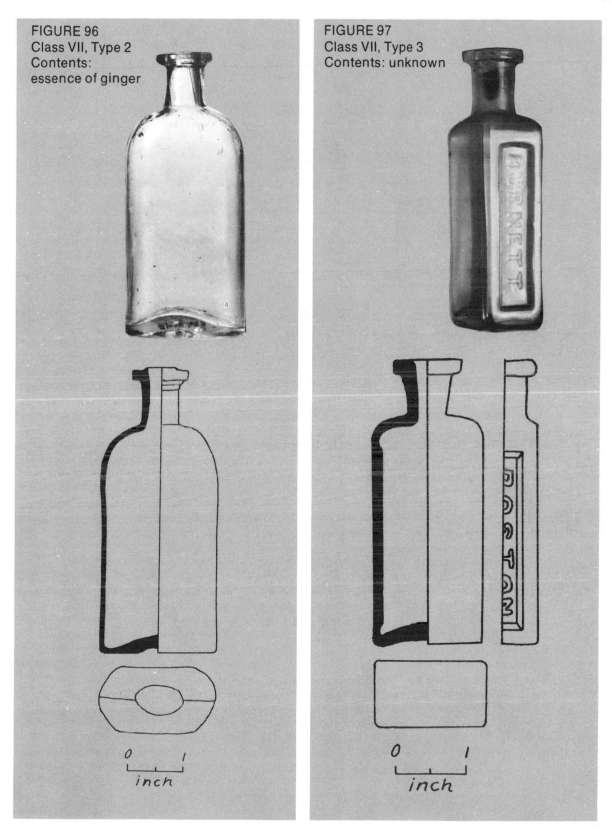

FIGURE 96
Class VII, Type 2
Contents:
essence of ginger

FIGURE 97
Class VII, Type 3
Contents: unknown

CLASS VII
CHEMICALS AND MEDICINE

Class VII, Type 1:

Only four 38-ounce-capacity, mold-blown chemical bottles were taken from the *Bertrand* cargo (Table 13). The bottles are cylindrical with slightly dished bases and rounded shoulders (fig. 95). The bottle necks are cylindrical, and terminate in 1/4-inch-wide collars with flat lips. Made in two-piece molds, the bottles are transparent aqua in color and stand 9 1/4 inches high. Each bottle is stoppered with a clear octagonal-topped pressed glass stopper made in a two-piece mold. The lower cylindrical part of each stopper has been ground smooth, giving a hazy translucent appearance to the glass. These specimens may at one time have contained acid for assaying ore. Dimensions : height, 9 1/4 inches; diameter of base, 3 3/4 inches; diameter of neck, (outside), 1 1/2 inches, (inside), 15/16 inch.

The crate which held the bottles in straw tow was stenciled: "CHALLENGE CHEM / _____U_____KEL & CO. // ST. LOUIS, MO."; "GLASS SIDE UP / G. P. DORRIS."

Class VII, Type 2:

The most abundant type of medicine bottle from the boat's cargo is represented by 133 "French oval" bottles and fragments (Table 13). These small, interesting specimens (fig. 96) contain "William Brown's Highly Concentrated Essence of Ginger." Blown in two-piece molds, they are 5 1/16 to 5 1/8 inches high and measure 1 5/16 inches by 2 1/8 inches at the base. They hold about 4 ounces. The bases of most of the bottles are flat, but some are pushed up slightly. They are pale transparent aqua in color and have rounded shoulders and cylindrical necks about 3/4 inch high. The neck finish consists of an applied prescription style collar which is slightly flared at the base and has a flat or gently rounded lip. The orifices are stoppered with corks, and most of the bottles exhibit fragments of paper labels on both the front and back sides in blue, white, green, yellow and pink. Although some of the lettering has disappeared, enough of each label remained to reconstruct the wording, which reads: "WM. BROWN'S / HIGHLY / CONCENTRATED / ESSENCE / OF / GINGER / Dosage - One to two teaspoonsful in glass / full of water. / PREPARED BY / D.B. SMITH / 223 Saratoga St. / Between PINE AND PEARL / NEW YORK." Dimensions: height, 5 1/4 inches; base, 2 1/8 BY 1 3/8 inches; diameter of neck (outside), 1 1/16 inches, (inside), 7/16 inch.

The two cases which held the bottles were stenciled, but the field notes do not indicate the placement of the words on the cases. The stenciling once appeared as: "7 DOZ 5 OZ. / ESSENCE GINGER"; "C. S. K. / ST. LOUIS, MO."

Class VII, Type 3:

Twenty small clear glass, letter paneled prescription or extract bottles were recovered from the *Bertrand*, the contents of which are unknown (Table 13). The rectangular bottles have flat bases and were made in a two-piece mold. Each bottle stands 3 15/16 inches high and the body measures 1 9/16 inches by 15/16 inch. The cylindrical neck is finished with a flat-lipped prescription collar. The sides of the bottle with the smallest dimensions bear recessed panels, one of which is lettered "BURNETT" and the other is lettered "BOSTON" (fig. 97). The cork-stoppered bottles presumably held an extract of some description or one of the cure-alls produced by Joseph Burnett, a well-known Boston chemist. Petsche (1972, personal communication) indicates that, according to his field notes, the bottles probably contained lemon extract, but because there is some doubt, and because of their prescription type morphology, they have been classed with chemicals and medicines. Dimensions: height, 3 15/16 inches; base, 1 9/16 by 15/16 inches; diameter of neck, (outside), 15/16 inch, (inside), 3/8 inch.

III

Bottle Makers
and their Marks

If it were simply a matter of identifying bottle makers of the mid-19th century by embossments on commercial bottles, this research effort would be more complete. Although anyone could afford to have a plate mold made for his product, this did not happen as often as the glass historian would like. Large commercial interests were not so interested in selling bottles as they were the products they contained. Plain bottles were cheaper to make and advertising could be affixed to them with paper labels.

Glassmaking by the middle of the 19th century was the economic mainstay of several eastern cities, and contributed significantly to the gross economic products of others. Unfortunately, the problem of attribution continues to plague us, because even the largest of the glass houses kept inadequate historical records concerning the volumes and varieties of bottles produced, and the nature of embossments and mold marks on their wares. It is disappointing that only a few 19th-century glass houses have been identified from mold marks on bottles from the Bertrand cargo. In the future, as more information becomes available, other bottle makers will be identified and added to those included in this chapter.

DENBY AND CODNER

The Denby and Codner Park Potteries owned by Joseph Bourne are probably most famous for brown, salt glazed, wheel thrown ink bottles they made for P. & J. Arnold of London. Although the Arnold firm is no longer in business, the Bourne Potteries near Derby continue to make fine stoneware of various kinds.

ELLENVILLE GLASS WORKS

In addition to the whiskey bottles produced at Willington, a few Bertrand examples are marked "ELLENVILLE GLASS WORKS." Founded in 1836 by a group of stockholders, some of whom were connected with the Willington Glass Company (Toulouse, 1971, p. 179), the plant was located in Ulster County, New York, on a canal connecting the Delaware and Hudson Rivers. By 1865, operating as the Ellenville Glass Company, the firm's assets totaled $368,000 in materials and finished articles. The McKearins (1971, p. 182) state that ownership of the company changed in 1866 and its name was modified to Ellenville Glass Works. Inasmuch as the Bertrand

71

bottles are marked Ellenville Glass Works, new molds were in use by 1864 or the changes in ownership that the McKearins suggest took place two years earlier than was once believed. At any rate, the company changed hands again in 1879 and thereafter it was known as the Ellenville Glass Factory (McKearin and McKearin, 1971, pp. 182, 602).

KENTUCKY GLASS WORKS

Neither the Schroeder's Spice Bitters nor the Schroeder's Stomach Bitters bottles in the *Bertrand* cargo were embossed on the bases with letters, but presumably they were products of the Kentucky Glass Works Company of Louisville. The firm was established in 1849 by Taylor, Stanger, Ramsey and Company and was sold the following year to George L. Douglass and James Taylor (McKearin and McKearin, 1971, p. 606; Toulouse, 1971, p. 323). The factory produced vials, demijohns and bottles of other kinds, including some made in private molds. By 1855 the factory had been purchased by Douglas, Rutherford & Company, and the name had been changed to Louisville Glass Works. Ownership of the Louisville Works changed again in 1856 and 1865 and thereafter about every two years until it closed in 1873. However, according to Toulouse (1971, p. 324) the shop was purchased and reopened that same year by Captain J. B. Ford, who operated it as the Louisville Kentucky Glass Works until about 1886.

There is no way to determine exactly when the Schroeder's bottles on the *Bertrand* were made. Between 1849 and 1855 the company used the marks "K Y G W," but it may have used others, including "KY G W Co," about which we have no information. By 1870, if not earier, their bottles were marked "L G W" to reflect the change in the company name in 1855. Inasmuch as the firm did considerable business in bottles made in private molds it is not unreasonable to assume the Schroeder's Spice Bitters bottles and the "French square" Schroeder's Stomach Bitters bottles are two such products.

Apparently the *Bertrand* specimens differ from the usual run of Schroeder's bottles in some other respects. Sold in quarts and pints, the "leg" shaped bottles are most commonly lettered on one side "SCHROEDER'S / BITTERS / LOUISVILLE, KY." The *Bertrand* examples are lettered "SCHROEDER'S SPICE / BITTERS."

LORENZ & WIGHTMAN

The initials "L & W" which appear on the bases of several Dr. J. Hostetter's bitters bottles belong to the "Lorenz and Wightman" firm of Pittsburgh. Of the two partners, the most is known about Frederick Lorenz. Lorenz was born in Germany and went to work in 1813 in Craig & O'Hara's Pittsburgh Glass Works. After O'Hara's death, Lorenz leased the plant and finally bought it and the Treavor & Ensell plant. In 1824 he built the Sligo Glass Works and the Temperanceville Glass Works, the latter of which produced window glass. In 1841, already in a partnership with Thomas Wightman, he entered into a partnership agreement with William McCully and A. W. Buchanan, and the four men consolidated their holdings under the firm name of "McCully & Co." After the dissolution of the four-way partnership in 1851, Lorenz and Wightman continued to operate the Pittsburgh Glass Works using the firm name "Lorenz & Wightman" until 1860. Fahnstock, Albree & Co. leased the works from 1860 to 1862, but defaulted and gave up the lease. The new Lorenz & Wightman Company formed after this date was owned and operated by Frederick's son, Moses Lorenz, Thomas Wightman, and W. K. Nimick until Moses died in 1871 and the firm was dissolved. Thereafter the business was known as "Thomas Wightman & Co."

In view of this history it is reasonable to assume that the second Lorenz & Wightman firm produced at least some bottles during the 1860's for David Hostetter, also of Pittsburgh.

WILLIAM McCULLY & COMPANY

One case of amber bottles marked "W McCULLY & CO / PITTSBURGH PA" on the bases and "PATENTED" on the shoulders, were taken from the steamer *Bertrand*. Although the bottles are of a type morphologically associated with whiskey, their contents include only four percent alcohol by volume, and the identity of the liquid remains unknown. In addition to the bottles, four dozen panes of window glass from the cargo are also known to have been produced by the McCully firm.

The history of the company which produced these particular bottles is nearly as complex as the bulk of this report. Irish born, William McCully learned glassblowing in Bakewell's Grant Street factory in Pittsburgh, and later worked for Frederick Lorenz in the "Pittsburgh Glass Works," where he became proficient in blowing cylinder window glass. In 1829 he began a partnership in Pittsburgh with Captain John Hay and built the "Union Flint Glass Works," which was destroyed by flood and fire in 1832. Though the partnership was dissolved, McCully rebuilt the plant later that year and named it the "Phoenix Glass Co." By 1840 he also had acquired two plants in the Williamsport area of Pittsburgh (Toulouse, 1971, pp. 351-352; McKearin and McKearin, 1971, p. 595).

McCully and another partner, A. W. Buchanan, formed a loose partnership with Frederick Lorenz, and his associate, Thomas Wightman, in 1841. Among the Lorenz holdings, in addition to the "Pittsburgh Glass Works," were the "Temperanceville Glass Works," and the "Sligo Glass Works" (McKearin and McKearin, 1971, pp. 594, 596). In 1851, when the partnership was dissolved, most of the holdings reverted to the former ownership, except that Lorenz sold the Sligo Glass Works to the continuing McCully & Co. William McCully died in 1859, but the firm was continued by his son John and several other partners who were added both before and after William's death.

Inasmuch as the raised letters on the bases of the *Bertrand* bottles are qualified with "Co," they had to have been blown after 1841, probably between 1856 and 1866, at the Phoenix Glass Co. (Toulouse, 1971, pp. 352-353).

WILLINGTON GLASS WORKS

Only a few of the bourbon whiskey cocktail bottles recovered from the *Bertrand* bear raised letters on their bases. Fortunately, several are marked "WILLINGTON GLASS WORKS," and represent the products of a well-known glass company.

The Willington Glass Company began operating in 1815 in West Willington, Connecticut, but little is known of its financial status until after 1847. Several stockholders in the company were associated with other Connecticut glass houses, some by close family ties. According to White (1941, p. 99), by 1849-1850 the plant had grown considerably and its owners may have been planning to open three shops. The Willington Glass Company was extremely successful for eight years following 1849, but it was caught in the bank panic of 1857, struggled through two depressions and the Civil War, and failed in 1872-1873, not having made glass for ten years.

Among the productions of the Willington works were demijohns, wine, whiskey, ale and bitters bottles, also flasks and Gothic or cathedral pickle bottles. The bottles were sold directly to product manufacturers or through dealers in several surrounding states. Although the possibility exists that some of the pickle bottles on the *Bertrand* were produced in the Willington Glass Works, business in Boston, where the pickles and fruits were packed, was noticeably lacking (White, 1941, p. 100).

IV

Manufacturers and Consignees

The names of several well-known individuals are associated with various products recovered from the *Bertrand*, but perhaps equally significant is the identification of little-known consumer product manufacturers and the nature of their contributions to American commercial history.

The remarkable growth of the West toward urban maturity did not come without the many improvements in transportation which laid the groundwork for economic expansion in western cities. As the population grew, manufacturing increased, and the center of urban power moved westward, from Boston to Philadelphia and Cincinnati, to Lexington, to St. Louis and beyond. With this movement went hundreds of thousands of energetic producers of finished goods. Those who did not choose to follow the tide of urban power used improved transportation such as steamboats to move their finished products to the West for sale and distribution. Perhaps, in that spirit, this chapter illuminates at least a few business personalities of the times and their far-reaching interests.

BITTERS, BOURBON AND WINE

Calvin A. Richards

One practically unknown retailer of the period, whose name is associated with whiskey and wine from the Bertrand cargo, was Calvin A. Richards. Boston City Directories (1861, 1867) list Richards as a retailer of wines, cigars and cigarettes at 91 Washington Street during the period between 1861 and 1867. He apparently retailed several brands of bitters in addition to bar goods. Dr. Abbott's Bitters, made by C. W. Abbott and Company, Baltimore, bearing a paper label with the signature of C. A. Richards, was one such product. Richards was also the proprietor of Richard's Sonoma Wine Bitters made from California grapes and "aromatic and healthful plants" (Watson, 1965, pp. 247, 270). His obituary in the *Boston Evening Transcript* for Tuesday, February 15, 1892, which appears below, indicates that, although he sold wines and liquors for a short time, he was successful in other business ventures, including real estate:

CALVIN A. RICHARDS DEAD.
✤ ✤ ✤ ✤ ✤ ✤ ✤ ✤

He Succumbs to Heart Disease About Noon—Sketch of His Career.

Calvin A. Richards died at his home 394 Beacon street today shortly after noon. Heart disease is the cause ascribed. At quarter before twelve he answered a telephone call from his office and within half an hour from that time he was dead. Mr. Richards was about sixty years of age. He was a member of the Common Council in 1858, 1859 and 1861, while in 1862 he was a member of the Board of Aldermen.

As a business man Mr. Richards had been very successful. He began with the manufacture of proprietary articles and with the money made this way he opened a liquor store on the corner of Washington street and Williams court, where he continued for a long time. His earnings he invested in real estate at the South End, including the Metropolitan Hotel. In 1874 he was induced to go into the board of direction of the Metropolitan Street Railroad and he in a short time succeeded President Draper. To take this responsible position Mr. Richards was induced to relinquish many business cases, and endeavor to ascertain if the old-time prestige of the valuable property could be recovered. The Highland Railroad had secured a franchise and was launched into immediate success. The energy at once displayed by Mr. Richards was felt in every department, and his direction was always noted for prompt, vigorous policy. After the Metropolitan was absorbed by the West End Railroad Mr. Richards became connected with the latter road as general manager under President Whitney, but after a few weeks in that position he resigned.

Mr. Richards was one of the largest owners of real estate in the city. For thirty years he has been a large investor in property from Dover street out, and he is believed to have been the largest single owner of real estate in that section. He also owned the John C. Paige building at No. 20 Kilby street and the Richards building at No. 114 Hate street. For about twenty years he was a resident of West Chester park, and for the last two years he had lived on Beacon street.

Mr. Richards was the son of L. D. Richards, who died a few years ago, and with whom he was a partner in the liquor business. He had a wife and one daughter, and his brother Henry also survives him.

The funeral services will be held at Mr. Richard's late residence, 394 Beacon street, Thursday noon. The burial will be private.

H. A. Richards

H. A. Richards, whose name and address appear on cases of Kelly's Old Cabin Bitters, may have been a brother or a cousin of Calvin Richards. No references to H. A. Richards were found in the Boston Public Library, indicating that he may have been in silent partnership with Calvin, although the addresses differ.

Dr. Jacob Hostetter

Of greater fame in the mid-19th century was Dr. Jacob Hostetter and his son David. Dr. Hostetter was a prominent Pennsylvania physician who, for a number of years, had prescribed a tonic of his own formulation for his patients. In 1853 David Hostetter adopted his father's prized prescription to concoct the famous "Hostetter Stomachic Bitters." The tonic was sold successfully under the trademark "Hostetter & Smith," registered under numbers 3, 135, 223 and 8,970 in the United States Patent Office between July 4, 1859, and December, 1884, when the trademark was changed to "Hostetter & Co." This same trademark, which incorporated the use of specific labels, was declared again on August 9, 1888 and was registered as Number 15,873 by the United States Patent Office on September 18, 1888. Between 1889 and 1920, the Hostetter Company was selling bitters all over the world, backed by an advertising campaign that cost $4,425,000 in the 30-year period. Most of the advertising took the form of regularly published almanacs.

The product contained 25 percent alcohol by volume, but this presumably was used only to extract the medicinal virtues of the plant materials it contained. The alcohol was also regarded as a solvent and preservative. The other active natural and synthetic ingredients the "Hostetter" formulation contained, and the volume in which they were present per fluid ounce, appear in an undated advertisement from the Hostetter Corporation (personal communication, A. B. Adams, Vice-president of the Hostetter Company). Ingredients cited in the Adams statement are listed below:

Cinchona bark (Cinchona succirubra)	15.00 grains
Centuary plant (Erythraea centarium)	0.65 grains
Anise fruit (Pimpinella anisum)	0.65 grains
Serpentaria Roots (Artistolocha serpentaria)	3.00 grains
Yerba Santa Leaves (Eriodictyon californicum)	2.00 grains
Calamus rhizomes (Acorus calamus)	2.00 grains
Culver's Roots (Veronica virginica)	0.42 grains
Ginger rhizomes (Zingiber officinale)	1.00 grains
Nux Vomica seed (Strychmos Nux vomica)	8.00 m.
Glycerine	5 %
Sugar not to exceed	20.00 grains
Saccharin	1/15 grain
Oil of Orange	0.5 m.

Nux vomica or strychnine is readily identifiable as a poisonous, colorless, crystalline alkaloid which is used in small doses as a stimulant to the nervous system. Cinchona bark is a bitter alkaloid with various medicinal properties; from it quinine is extracted. Anise is a small white or yellow flowered plant of the carrot family whose seed is used primarily as a flavoring, while calamus, sometimes called "sweet flag" is a palm-like plant. The purpose of the latter in the formula is not known. Ginger, of course, is a tropical herb whose rootstalk is used as a flavoring and in medicines. The other ingredients need no explanation.

Regardless of the ingredients, even teetotalers found stimulation in the cure-all, and it became exceedingly popular both in the North and the South prior to the Civil War. The *South Carolina Banner* of May 6, 1858, printed in Abbeville, contained the following Hostetter's advertisement:

> A wine-glass full of these Bitters taken three times a day, will be a sure cure for Dyspepsia, will remove all flatulency; assist digestion; give a good appetite, and impart a healthy tone to the whole system, and is a certain preventive of fever and ague. Children, delicate ladies, or persons in a debilitated state should try a bottle.

The U.S. Army abolished the liquor ration for troops in 1832. When the Civil War began, Hostetter and other makers of patent medicines urged their products on the Federal government for use by the military. Hostetter deplored the use of common whiskey by officers in the field, believing that his concoction of bitters was better for their health and morals (Carson, 1961, p. 49; Lord, 1969, p. 52). His advice on the subject of bitters was doubtless followed with enthusiasm by northern soldiers, a condition which more than made up for the loss of most of his southern market.

When alcohol was allocated during World War I, Hostetter and Company suffered severe financial difficulties from which it never fully recovered. However, in 1902 Hostetter was listed as one of 3,045 certified millionaires in the United States, and is said to have made something in excess of $18 million from his celebrated tonic (Carson, 1961, pp. 42, 73).

In 1959 the State Pharmacal Company of Newark, New Jersey, a wholly owned division of Hazel Bishop Incorporated, Union, New Jersey, purchased the trademark and business of Dr. Hostetter's Stomachic Bitters. The trademark is still owned by that firm and is listed by the United States Patent Office under Serial Number 76,604, filed June 26, 1959 and registered May 24, 1960 (No. 698,028); the product is no longer made.

Colonel P. H. Drake

Another famous name in proprietary medicines of the 1860's and represented in the *Bertrand* cargo is that of Colonel P. H. Drake. If Colonel Drake's Plantation Bitters looked and tasted like whiskey, it was because it was just that, or, more specifically, St. Croix rum (Carson, 1961, p. 45). This "nutritious" essence, which was derived from sugar cane and bittered with barks and herbs, made its appearance during the Civil War when there was a high excise tax on whiskey.

Colonel Drake is said to have spent a great deal of money on advertising and went to great lengths to promote his product. His mysterious advertising jargon containing the letters and figures "S. T. 1860 X" appeared on fences, barns, billboards and rocks around the world. Drake, as some historians have it, even tried to paint his slogan on Mount Ararat, Niagara Falls, and on the famous Egyptian pyramids, but he was unsuccessful in all three ventures (Carson, 1961, pp. 42, 92).

J. H. Schroeder

Not a great deal is known about J. H. Schroeder, other than the fact that he produced bitters, probably made with catawba wine. He was a dealer in wines, liquors and general bar stores. The *Louisville Business Mirror* for 1858-1859 (p. 281) includes an advertisement for the Schroeder business. Louisville printed no directories during the Civil War, but by 1864 the firm was again listed on Wall Street as "J. H. Schroeder and Son." In 1865 the business moved to Main Street, Louisville (Martin F. Schmidt., Louisville Free Public Library, personal communication, 1971).

FOODSTUFFS

William Underwood

Most fresh fruits and some vegetables were commodities that western storekeepers in the 19th century did not stock; there were none on the market. Most of these products were sold either in dried form or in cans or bottles. One quite famous canner's products are recorded in the *Bertrand* cargo—those of William Underwood Company. This year (1972) marks the 150th year of business for the Underwood firm, which produced some of the canned peaches, jelly and preserves, pickles, and bottles of catsup found on the steamer *Bertrand*.

The Underwood business was founded in 1822 by William Underwood, a partner in the firm until 1864. His son, William James Underwood, became associated with him in 1851. Underwood had served his apprenticeship in pickling and food preserving in London before coming to the United States to start his cannery in Boston. By about 1825 he was shipping bottled fruits to South America and the Far East. The company continued to bottle most of its products until 1846 when lobster canning began at branch plants in Maine. As early as the 1820's, Underwood was bottling milk with sugar for use on seagoing ships, and for shipment to South America. Among the remaining bottled perishables the firm produced were sauces, mustard, cranberries without sugar, preserves, including cranberry jam, spiced meats, and pie fruits.

In the mid-1830's, Underwood imported tomato plants from England and began raising tomatoes to can. Each hermetically sealed bottle of tomatoes contained the "substance" of about two dozen tomatoes which were cooked slowly to evaporate the water particles after first having been strained to remove the skins and seeds. A number of bottles of Underwood's catsup were recovered from the *Bertrand*. Unfortunately none retained labels. These, and the canned peaches, were probably purchased from Numsen, Carroll, Inc., 18 Light St., Baltimore by Charles S. Kintzing, a St. Louis wholesaler, or they were wholesaled by an Underwood and Company branch office in St. Louis. One crate is stenciled "UNDERWOOD & CO. / TOMATOE KETCHUP / 67 BROAD STREET / ST. LOUIS, MO." and several cases of canned peaches also make reference to St. Louis.

Inasmuch as most of the glass bottles purchased by Underwood came from the Ellenville Glass Company, it is not unreasonable to assume that at least some of the *Bertrand* specimens are from this source.

W. K. Lewis

A large number of lettered foil seals were found covering the corks on pickle bottles and brandied peach bottles. Many were marked "*W. K. LEWIS & BROTHERS*/ PRESERVES / PICKLES / SEAL'D MEATS & c. / BOSTON." which can be attributed to the W. K. Lewis who operated as a canner in Boston during the 1850's and the 1860's and established the term "baked" beans in the canner's glossary.

MEDICINES AND EXTRACTS

Joseph Burnett

The name "BURNETT / BOSTON" found on 20 small rectangular lettered panel medicine bottles, and on one case of lemon extract, could be no other person but Joseph Burnett, a Boston chemist who formulated a popular asthma cure and a number of other household remedies in the 1840's. Burnett's inventive genius produced the first vanilla extract sold in this country in 1847 (Johnson, 1961, pp. 61, 62, P1. 58).

SAUCES

Lea and Perrins

Lea and Perrins is not an unfamiliar name to those who like Worcestershire sauce, nor was it uncommon to Americans early in the 19th century. Thirty-three Lea & Perrins sauce bottles and fragments taken from the *Bertrand* definitely represent an imported product. Mr. Ransom H. Duncan, Technical Director of Lea and Perrins, Inc., who is in the fifth generation of the Duncan family connected with the manufacture and sale of the sauce, has contributed much to our knowledge of the company.

Lea & Perrins sauce was introduced to the United States from Worcester, England, in the late 1830's or early 1840's. It was imported to this country by John Duncan's Sons, New York, until 1877. In this year the Duncans began producing Worcestershire sauce in their own plant in New York. The bottles bearing glass stoppers embossed "LEA & PERRINS" from the Bertrand cargo may not have been produced in England, as the English bottles were embossed vertically up the side "LEA & PERRINS," and not "E. F. DIXIE CO." as on the Bertrand specimens. Lea & Perrins' bottles after 1880 were also embossed on the bases "J / D / S" and bore a mold number. Prior to that date they were embossed "A B C Co" on the bases. The bottles were labeled with orange-on-black front labels and black-on-white back labels, overwrapped with a piece of parchment-type paper tied at the necks with red string and sealed with a red wax seal bearing the words "LEA & PERRINS WORCESTERSHIRE SAUCE." The Bertrand specimens provide no evidence of labels or wrappers, and exhibit no embossing on their bases. Mr. Duncan believes that the "E.F. DIXIE" embossing may represent an early patent infringement (personal communication, 1971).

INK

R. B. Snow

Not much is known concerning one of the names associated with Bertrand ink bottles. R. B. Snow is listed in *Campbell & Richardson's St. Louis Business Directory* for 1863 (L. Harrington, Missouri Historical Society, personal communication, 1971) as "R. B. SNOW & PHILIP J HELGENBERG," wholesalers of drugs. Their establishment was located on Main Street at the northwest corner of Vine. The St. Louis Directory for 1864 (Alma Vaughan, State Historical Society of Missouri, personal communication, 1971) lists Snow at the same address, but without a partner.

P. & J. Arnold

P. & J. Arnold inks were very well known on the American frontier. Arnold produced writing and duplicating inks which were sold in bulk stoneware containers made by the Joseph Bourne Pottery. P. & J. Arnold produced quality duplicating and writing inks in several colors between 1724 and 1950 when the business closed. However, the Bourne Pottery, according to Wilson (1974, In Press) continues to make pottery products.

CONSIGNEES

Francis Lyman Worden

Inasmuch as merchandising and freighting were sources of considerable income for enterprising investors in Montana, it is not unusual to find stenciled on Bertrand cargo the names of men engaged in these businesses. Perhaps the best known merchant represented is Francis (Frank) Lyman Worden. A considerable number of goods from the *Bertrand* are consigned to "Worden & Co., Hell Gate, M. T." or simply to "Worden, Hell Gate, M. T."

Frank Worden and his partner, Captain Christopher P. Higgins, became two of the most prosperous men in the territory after 1860 when they founded Wordensville and built a grist mill and a saw mill there. The merchandising business they founded earlier at Hell Gate was moved to Wordensville and was so successful that they later confined their enterprises there. Subsequently, Worden renamed the town Missoula. Perhaps the best description of Worden is contained in the biography written in 1896 by Wilbur F. Sanders for the Historical Society of Montana (1896, pp. 362-364).

Prior to his association with Worden, Higgins was a packer and wagon freight expert in the party of Lieutenant John Mullan, an engineer who surveyed the "Mullen" military road between Fort Benton and Walla Walla, Washington, between 1853 and 1859.

Granville Stuart

Stencils reading "Stuart and Co., Deer Lodge, M. T." refer to consignments for Granville Stuart and his brother James. Granville was, besides early Montana's most articulate cattle king, a merchant of great talent who capitalized on the unique economic conditions around Deer Lodge in the 1860's. He owned interests in gold mines, general merchandising, and trading. Later, he became a cattle baron and was one of the early legislators of the Territory.

As young men in the late 1850's, he and his brother James had a small trading business and also occupied themselves with a little prospecting. Later they founded American Fork on Benetsee Creek and sluiced gold with some results.

By 1862 the Stuarts, now accompanied by their brother Tom, had begun a mining operation in the Deer Lodge Valley, but divided their time between farming, trading and mining. According to Petsche (1974), Granville was advertising in local newspapers in 1865 as a dealer in dry goods, groceries, hardware, cutlery, boots, shoes, hats, and clothing. In the 1870's and 1880's Granville Stuart became the most successful cattleman in the western valleys of the territory (Fletcher, 1961, pp. 22-28).

John T. Murphy

John T. Murphy was another of the consignees reported from stenciling on the *Bertrand* cargo. Murphy was born in Missouri in 1842, and as a young man clerked and kept store in Colorado. In 1864 he brought a wagon load of goods from Colorado to the busy mining camp of Virginia City. This venture was so successful that, in the late spring of 1865, he shipped a large volume of goods up the Missouri by steamer to Fort Benton and overland from there to Helena. This daring act apparently sparked his eminant success as a Montana businessman, but we can only speculate how large his losses were when the goods consigned to him succumbed with the *Bertrand* earlier in the spring of the year. From Helena, Murphy's retail and wholesale grocery business branched out to Deer Lodge and Fort Benton. Taking a partner, Murphy, Neel and Co. expanded their interests to include freighting, most of which was conducted from warehouses at Fort Benton. By 1886, according to Petsche (1974), Murphy had merged with Frank Worden of Missoula, and in 1890 he sold his Helena store and helped organize the Helena National Bank. Murphy-Maclay Hardware Co. of Great Falls bears his name to this day (Armitage, 1961: 66).

General G. P. Dorris

Practically nothing is known of G. P. Dorris, to whom chemicals and mining supplies were consigned. Petsche (1974) reports that General Dorris was a pioneer merchant in Virginia City, who, in addition to other mining supplies, stocked clothing especially made for miners.

V

Conclusions

Fortunately, most bottles can be grouped in categories descriptive of their use. The abundance and variety of bottles on the steamer *Bertrand* not only gives testimony to the quality of life on the American frontier in 1865, it also provides some subtle information by which the economic and social conditions of the period can be interpreted.

It is well known that the influx of prospectors and adventurers into Montana Territory was so great that shortages of supplies and equipment were common (Petsche, 1974). However, despite high transportation costs, losses to the river, and the imminent risk of their goods being captured by Indians, frontier merchants kept, or at least tried to keep, stocks of goods in adequate volume and variety to meet the ever-growing demands. Nevertheless, their confessed objective was money, and lists of over-the-counter prices in the remote and "uncivilized" western territories during the 1860's would seem to reflect that money was plentiful and that people were getting rich fast. The vender's main clientele were miners, and a few ranchers, sodbusters and travelers. Their very presence only contributed to the shortages in goods, and to an inflationary trend in which gold dust was the circulating currency, and greenbacks were taken at eighty cents on the dollar (Upham, 1962, pp. 285-286).

Staple foods such as flour, sugar, potatoes, beans, hominy, butter, bacon and tea appear to have been consistently in short supply. Under these circumstances, one is inclined to agree with Petsche (1974) that "whatever else might have been in the holds of the *Bertrand*, she was carrying goods that would have substantially alleviated such food shortages." The wreck of the steamer was a serious matter, not just to the consumer, but to the boat owners and shippers of goods as well. However, profit margins were high on cargoes that did reach Fort Benton, and monetary losses to owners and shippers resulting from wrecks were at least partially recouped through insurance. A good indication of just how high profit margins were in 1865 is reflected in a letter from a merchant and passenger on the steamer *Twilight* to a friend in which he projected a profit of 6000 percent on the stock he had purchased in St. Louis (Upham, 1962, p. 283).

Judging from newspaper accounts, letters, ledgers, and catalogues of the period, canned goods were slightly cheaper than bottled products immediately after the Civil War. The *Montana Post*, April 23, 1865, advertised canned sardines at 50 cents a can, tinned fruits for $1.05 per can, and oysters at $1.25. However, this is a book about bottles, and bottled goods certainly were very much in evidence everywhere at this time. Perhaps the most representative data on the retail prices of bottled goods in the 1860's is found in the ledger kept by Seth E. Ward, post trader at Fort Laramie, Wyoming, between 1858 and 1872. Mr. Ward's records for the period from 1866 to 1870 are abstracted below to indicate the price per bottle paid by consumers. Only those products found on the *Bertrand,* or those of comparable identity, are listed. The capacities of most bottles are not known.

1866

Ale $1.00
Wine 3.50-5.00
Champagne 5.00
Whiskey . . . . .1.75 qt.
. . . . .1.25 pt.
Bourbon 3.50
Cognac 3.50
Brandy cocktail 2.50
Best brandy .5.00
Bitters 2.00
Schnapps 2.50
Brandied peaches 2.50
Catsup 75
Pepper sauce .50
London Sauce 1.25
Club Sauce .1.25
Lemon syrup 1.00
Horseradish .1.00
Castor oil 35
Olive oil 2.00
Black ink 35
Indelible ink .75
Red ink 75
Essence of ginger 75
Patent medicine 1.50
French mustard 75
Pickled onions 1.50
Worcester sauce . . . . .2.50 large

1867

Stomach bitters 1.50
Schiedam Schnapps 3.00
Gin . . . . .1.50 pt.
Brandied cherries 2.50
Pickles 1.50
Castor oil 50
Piccalilli 1.25
Molasses . . . . .1.50 1/2 gal.
Worcester sauce . . . . .1.25 small
Lemon extract 75
Cayenne pepper 75
Arnold's writing fluid 2.50

1868

Brandy cocktail 2.50
Burnett vanilla 75

1869

Catawba wine 1.50
Imported wine 4.00

1870

Pickled oysters 1.00

It is unfortunate that so few records remain concerning the *Bertrand,* her cargo and passengers. Lacking shipping manifests, journals, diaries, and other documents, there are obvious gaps in the information presented. However, from the study of the bottles has come a body of information which may be useful to others in translating the details of American life in other historic times and places.

References

Armitage, George T.
　1961　"Prelude to the Last Round-up: the Dying Days of the Great 79," *Montana*, vol 11, no. 4. Historical Society of Montana, Helena.

Arnold, John P.
　1933.　*History of the Brewing Industry and Brewing Science in America*. G. L. Peterson. Chicago.

Boston City Directory
　1861.　Boston.
　1867.　Boston.

Boston Evening Transcript
　1892.　"Calvin A. Richards Dead." Tuesday, February 15. Boston.

Brill, Robert H.
　1962.　"A Note on a Scientist's Classification of Glass," *Journal of Glass Studies*, vol. 4. The Corning Museum of Glass, Corning Glass Center. Corning.

Carson, Gerald
　1961.　*One for a Man, Two for a Horse*. Bramhall House, Clarkson N. Potter, Inc. New York.

Chittenden, Capt. Hiram Martin
　1970.　"Report on Steamboat Wrecks on the Missouri River," *Nebraska History*, vol. 51, no. 1. Nebraska State Historical Society. Lincoln.

　1962.　*History of Early Steamboat Navigation on the Missouri River: Life and Adventures of Joseph La Barge, Pioneer Navigator and Indian Trader for Fifty Years, Identified with the Commerce of the Missouri Valley*, vol. 1. Ross & Haines, Inc. Minneapolis.

D'Amato, Susan E.
　1971.　"A Descriptive Account of the Textiles Recovered from the Steamboat Bertrand." Manuscript on file at Midwest Archeological Center, National Park Service. Lincoln.

Encyclopedia Britannica
　1949.　Glass. vol. 10.

Ferraro, Pat, and Bob Ferraro
　1966.　*A Bottle Collector's Book*. Western Printing and Publishing Company. Sparks, Nevada.

Fletcher, Robert H.
1961.   "The Day of the Cattlemen Dawned Early—In Montana." *Montana*, vol. 11, no. 4. Historical Society of Montana. Helena.

Holscher, H. H.
1965.   "Hollow and Specialty Glass: Background and Challenge." Reprint by Owens-Illinois of Toledo, Ohio; initially appearing in *The Glass Industry*, vol. 46, June-November. Glass Publishing Company, Inc. New York.

Hunt, Charles B.
1959.   "Dating Mining Camps with Tin Cans and Bottles," *Geo Times*, vol. 3, no. 8. Geological Institute. Washington.

Johnson, Laurence A.
1961.   *Over the Counter and on the Shelf.* Bonanza Books, Crown Publishers, Inc. by agreement with Charles E. Tuttle Co., Inc. New York. (Printed in Japan)

Lavender, David
1965.   *The American Heritage History of the Great West.* Edited by Alvin M. Josephy, Jr. American Heritage Publishing Company, Incorporated. New York.

Lorrain, Dessamae
1968.   "An Archaeologist's Guide to Nineteenth Century American Glass," *Historical Archaeology*, vol. 2. The Society for Historical Archaeology.

Lord, Francis A.
1969.   *Civil War Sutlers and Their Wares.* Thomas Yoseloff. New York.

Louisville City Directory and Business Mirror
1858-59.   Hurd & Burrows, Publishers. Louisville.

McKearin, George S. and Helen McKearin
1971.   *American Glass.* Crown Publishers, Inc. New York

1950.   *Two Hundred Years of American Blown Glass.* Crown Publishers, Inc. New York.

Montana Post
1865.   April 23. (Virginia City, M.T.)

Moore, N. Hudson
1924.   *Old Glass, European and American.* Frederick A. Stoles Company. New York.

Petsche, Jerome E.
1974.   *The Steamboat Bertrand: History, Excavation and Architecture.* Office of Archeology and Historic Preservation, National Park Service. Washington, D.C.
1970.   "Uncovering the Steamboat Bertrand," *Nebraska History*, vol. 51, no. 1, Nebraska State Historical Society. Lincoln.

Sanders, Wilbur F.
1896.   "Francis Lyman Worden," *Contributions to the Historical Society of Montana; with its Transactions, Act of Incorporation, Constitution, Ordinances*, vol. 2. State Publishing Company, State Printers and Binders. Helena.

Schweiger, Catherine M.
1971.   "Techniques for Analysis of Dyes on Historic Textiles," M.S. Thesis, Graduate College, Department of Textiles, Clothing and Design, University of Nebraska. Lincoln.

South Carolina Banner
1858.   Hostetter's advertisement, May 6. (Abbeville.)

Switzer, Ronald R.
1972.   "Butcher Knives as Historical Sources," *The Museum of the Fur Trade Quarterly*, vol. 8, no. 1. The Museum of the Fur Trade. Chadron.
1972.   "Tally Ho's from the Steamboat Bertrand," *Just But-*

tons, vol. 30, no. 4. Just Buttons Museum. Southington.

1971. "Charles Parker's Britannia on the Steamboat Bertrand," *The Museum of the Fur Trade Quarterly,* vol. 7, no. 4. The Museum of the Fur Trade. Chadron.

1970. "Lead Bars from the St. Louis Shot Tower," *The Museum of the Fur Trade Quarterly,* vol. 6, no. 4. The Museum of the Fur Trade. Chadron.

Toulouse, Julian Harrison
1971. *Bottle Makers and Their Marks.* Thomas Nelson, Inc. New York.

Upham, Hiram D.
1962. "Upham Letters From the Upper Missouri, 1865," *Frontier Omnibus.* Edited by John W. Hakola, Historical Society of Montana. Montana State University Press. Missoula.

Ward, Seth E.
1866-70. Post Trader's ledger 1858-72; on file Wyoming State Archives. Cheyenne.

Watson, Richard
1965. *Bitters Bottles.* Thomas Nelson & Sons. New York.

Webster's New Twentieth Century Dictionary of the English Language
1964. (Unabridged), Second Edition. The World Publishing Company. Cleveland and New York.

Whitall, Tatum & Co. 1880
1971. American Historical Catalogue Collection. The Pyne Press. Princeton.

White, Henry Hall
1941. "The Willington Glass Company," *Antiques Magazine* vol. 40, no. 2.

Wilson, Rex L.
1974. *Bottles on the Western Frontier.* University of Arizona Press. Tucson.

1961. "A Classification System for 19th Century Bottles," *Arizoniana,* vol. 2, no. 4.

1961. "A Descriptive Analysis of Bottles from Fort Laramie." Unpublished manuscript, on file, Fort Laramie National Historic Site, Fort Laramie, Wyoming.

Appendix

TABLES

TABLE 1—Key to descriptive morphology applied to summaries of classes, types, and subtypes presented in tables 2 through 13.

	Base	Body	Shoulder	Neck
Vertical cross-section	a. flat	a. cylindrical	a. none	a. cylindrical
	b. convex	b. oval	b. conical	b. conical
	c. concave	c. pyramidal	c. tiered	c. bulbous
	d. lenticular	d. conical	d. stepped	d. banded
	e. beveled edge	e. expanding from base	e. pyramidal	e. ornate
		f. contracting from base	f. domed	f. none
		g. anthropomorphic effigy		
		h. zoomorphic effigy		
		i. representation of inanimate objects		
Horizontal cross-section	f. round	j. round	g. round	g. round
	g. oval	k. oval	h. oval	h. oval
	h. triangular	l. triangular	i. triangular	i. triangular
	i. rectangular	m. rectangular	j. rectangular	j. rectangular
	j. square	n. square	k. square	k. square
	k. pentagonal	o. pentagonal	l. pentagonal	l. pentagonal
	l. hexagonal	p. hexagonal	m. hexagonal	m. hexagonal
	m. octagonal	q. octagonal	n. octagonal	n. octagonal
	n. 10-sided	r. 10-sided	o. 10-sided	o. 10-sided
	o. 12-sided	s. 12-sided	p. 12-sided	p. 12-sided
	p. polygonal	t. polygonal	q. polygonal	q. polygonal
	q. irregular	u. irregular	r. irregular	r. irregular
		v. paneled	s. paneled	s. fluted
		w. fluted	t. fluted	t. other
Distinctive markings	r. impressed stamp	x. other	u. other	
	s. relief	y. impressed stamp	v. impressed stamp	u. rough where finish applied
	t. mold marks	z. relief	w. relief	v. mold marks
	u. pontil scar	aa. mold marks	x. mold marks	w. other
		bb. rotated in mold	y. ornate	
		cc. ornate		
		dd. other		

Material	1. Earthenware	2. Glass
	a. glazed	a. transparent
	b. unglazed	b. translucent
		c. opaque
		d. opalescent
		e. bubbly
		f. other

Color	1. amber and gold		6. crystal	
	2. black		7. green	
	3. blue and aqua		8. amethyst	
	4. brown		9. white	
	5. crockery		10. wine	

Stoppers and bails	a. glass	e. coal tar	j. thick foil seal (plain)	l. paper stamp (tax, etc.)
	b. glass and cork	f. string ties	k. thick foil seal (embellished)	m. other
	c. cork (plain)	g. wire bail		
	d. cork (embellished)	h. clamp bail		
		i. thin foil wrapper		

TABLE 2—Class I (Types 1 and 2) bottle features.

General description	1 ale-ceramic	1a ale-ceramic	1b ale-ceramic	1c ale-ceramic	1d ale-ceramic	1e ale-ceramic	1f ale-ceramic	1g ale-ceramic	2 Amsterdam ale-
Shape and distinctive markings									
Base:									
Vertical cross-section	a	a	ae	ae	ae	a	ae	ae	a
Horizontal cross-section	f	f	f	f	f	f	f	f	f
Markings									
Body:									
Vertical cross-section	ae	a	ae	a	ae	a	a	a	a
Horizontal cross-section	j	j	j	j	j	j	j	j	j
Markings	y	y	y	y	y	y			y
Shoulder:									
Vertical cross-section	b	b	b	b	b	f	f	b	b
Horizontal cross-section	g	g	g	g	g	g	g	g	g
Markings									
Neck:									
Vertical cross-section	b	b	b	b	b	b	b	b	a
Horizontal cross-section	g	g	g	g	g	g	g	g	g
Markings									
Neck finish (see fig. 2)	12	33	7	33	33	33	33	35	4
Material	1a	1a	1a	1a	1a	1a	1a	1a	1b
Color	1,5	1,5	1,5	1,5	1,5	1,5	1,5	1,5	4
Dimensions (in inches)									
Height:									
Base to shoulder	4-3/16	4-3/16	4-7/8	4-11/16	5-1/16	6-1/8	4-3/16	5-3/	8
Shoulder to neck terminus	3-13/16	3-15/16	2-3/4	2-11/16	2-7/8	3-5/8	3-5/16	3-7/8	2-1/2
Diameter of base	2-15/16	2-7/8	2-13/16	2-7/8	2-7/8	3-1/2	3	2-15/16	3-1/2
Diameter of neck:									
Outside	1-3/16	1-1/16	1	1-1/16	1-3/16	1	7/8	1-1/8	1-1/16
Inside	3/4	5/8	5/8	3/4	11/16	5/8	5/8	5/8	sealed
Capacity to brim (in ounces)	12-2/3	12-2/3	14-1/2	14	13-1/2	sealed	12-1/2	13	approx 32
Label	none	none	none	none	none	relief	none	none	yes
Stopper	cgi	cgi	cgi	cgi	cgi	cgi	cgi	cgi	ck
Case marks	none	none	none	none	none	none	none	none	yes

Distinctive features: Type 1, stamped with letters I, D, W, S, L, N, M; Subtype 1a, collar has sharp basal edge, Subtype 1b, stamped with L, C, M; Subtype 1e, stamped with "Price Bristol."

TABLE 3—Class I (Types 3 and 4) bottle features.

	Types and Subtypes								
	3	3a	3b	3c	3d	3e	3f	3g	4
General description	ale-glass	ale-glass	ale-glass	ale-glass	ale-glass	ale-glass	ale-glass	ale-glass	ale-glass
Shape and distinctive markings									
Base:									
Vertical cross-section	c	ce	c	c	ce	c	ce	c	c
Horizontal cross-section	f	f	f	f	f	f	f	f	f
Markings		s			s				
Body:									
Vertical cross-section	a	a	a	ae	ae	ae	ae	a	a
Horizontal cross-section	j	j	j	j	j	j	j	j	j
Markings	bb	bb			aa			bb	z,aa
Shoulder:									
Vertical cross-section	f	f	f	f	f	f	f	f	f
Horizontal cross-section	g	g	g	g	g	g	g	g	g
Markings		x	x	x	x	x	x		x
Neck:									
Vertical cross-section	c	b	c	c	c	c	c	c	c
Horizontal cross-section	g	g	g	g	g	g	g	g	g
Markings		u	u		u	u	u		
Neck finish (see fig. 2)	18	7	3	18	32	33	7	18	18
Material	2ae	2ae	2ce	2ce	2ae	2ae	2ae	2ce	2a
Color	1	1	2	2	1	1	1	2	1
Dimensions (in inches)									
Height:									
Base to shoulder	4-1/16	4-3/8	4-5/8	4	5	4-1/4	4-3/8	4-3/8	4-3/4
Shoulder to neck terminus ...	4-1/16	3-5/8	4	4-3/4	4-7/16	4-5/8	4-1/4	4-9/16	4-3/4
Diameter of base	3	2-13/16	2-9/16	2-15/16	2-1/2	2-3/4	2-11/16	2-15/16	2-9/16
Diameter of neck:									
Outside	7/8	1	1	7/8	1-1/16	15/16	1	7/8	1
Inside	11/16	13/16	3/4	5/8	11/16	3/4	3/4	11/16	3/4
Capacity to brim (in ounces) ...	12-3/4	14	12-1/3	13	14	ca. 14	14	15	14
Label	none	none	none	none	none	none	none	none	relief
Stopper	cgi	cgi	cgi	cgi	cgi	cgi	cgi	cgi	cgi
Case marks	yes	yes	yes	yes	yes	yes	yes	yes	yes

Distinctive features: Type 3, deep basal kick-up; Subtype 3b, knob on base center; Subtype 3c, knob on base center; Subtype 3e, knob on base center; Subtype 3f, knob on center of basal kick-up; Subtype 3g, deep basal kick-up.

TABLE 4—Class III (Types 1 and 2) bottle features.

	Type and Subtypes						
	1	1a	2	2a	2b	2c	2d
General description	wine demi-john	wine demi-john	cham-pagne	cham-pagne	cham-pagne split	cham-pagne split	cham-pagne split
Shape and distinctive markings							
Base:							
Vertical cross-section	c	c	c	c	c	c	c
Horizontal cross-section	f	f	f	f	f	f	f
Markings	t	t					
Body:							
Vertical cross-section	a	a	a	a	a	a	a
Horizontal cross-section	j	j	j	j	j	j	j
Markings			bb	bb	bb	bb	aa
Shoulder:							
Vertical cross-section	f	f	b	b	b	b	b
Horizontal cross-section	g	g	g	g	g	g	g
Markings							
Neck:							
Vertical cross-section	b	b	b	b	b	b	b
Horizontal cross-section	g	g	g	g	g	g	g
Markings							
Neck finish (see fig. 2)	1	1	13	13	13	13	13
Material	2ae	2be	2a	2a	2a	2a	2a
Color	3	7	7	7	7	7	7
Dimensions (in inches)							
Height:							
Base to shoulder	10		4-1/2	4-1/2	4	3-5/8	3-5/8
Shoulder to neck terminus ...	8		7-7/16	7-7/8	5-3/4	5-5/8	5-5/8
Diameter of base	7-1/2	7-5/8	3-11/16	3-3/4	3	3	2-15/16
Diameter of neck:							
Outside	1-5/8	1-9/16	15/16	1-1/8	13/16	13/16	13/16
Inside	7/8	1-1/4	3/4	13/16	3/4	3/4	3/4
Capacity to brim (in ounces) ...	384	384?	29	29	13-1/2	13-1/2	13-1/2
Label	none	none	none	none	yes	yes	yes
Stopper	c	c	cfghik	cfghik	cgiklm	cgiklm	cgikl
Case marks	none	none	yes	yes	yes	yes	yes

Distinctive features: Type 1, wicker covered; Type 2, knob on center of basal kick-up; Subtype 2b, knob on center of basal kick-up; Subtype 2d, knob on basal kick-up.

TABLE 5—Class III (Types 3, 4 and 5) bottle features.

	3	4	4a	4b	4c	5
			Types and Subtypes			
General description	wine	bourbon	bourbon	bourbon	bourbon?	brandy
Shape and distinctive markings						
Base:						
Vertical cross-section	c	c	c	c	c	c
Horizontal cross-section	f	f	f	f	f	f
Markings			s	s	s	s
Body:						
Vertical cross-section	ae	ae	ae	ae	ae	ae
Horizontal cross-section	j	j	j	j	j	j
Markings			z	z	bb	
Shoulder:						
Vertical cross-section	f	f	f	f	f	f
Horizontal cross-section	g	g	g	g	g	g
Markings		x			wx	x
Neck:						
Vertical cross-section	a	b	b	b	b	b
Horizontal cross-section	g	g	g	g	g	g
Markings						
Neck finish (see fig. 2)	9	7	7	7	7	18
Material	2ae	2ae	2ae	2ae	2ae	2ae
Color	7	1,7	1,7	1,7	1	1,7
Dimensions (in inches)						
Height:						
Base to shoulder	6-7/8	6-5/16	6	6	5-13/16	4-5/8
Shoulder to neck terminus	4-5/8	5-3/16	5-15/16	5-3/8	5-1/8	5-3/16
Diameter of base	2-7/8	3-1/16	3-1/8	3-1/8	2-13/16	3-11/16
Diameter of neck:						
Outside	1-1/8	1	1	1	1	1
Inside	7/8	3/4	3/4	7/8	3/4	3/4
Capacity to brim (in ounces)	25-1/2	25	25	25	21-1/2	25-1/2
Label	none	none	none	none	none	none
Stopper	ck	c	c	c	c	cgi
Case marks	none	yes	yes	yes	yes	none

Distinctive features: Type 4, knob on base center; Subtype 4a, "Willington Glass Works" on base; Subtype 4b, "Ellenville Glass Works" on base; Subtype 4c, "W. McCully & Co./Pittsburgh, Pa." on base.

TABLE 6—Class III (Type 6) bottle features.

General description	6 Hostetter's Bitters	6a Hostetter's Bitters	6b Hostetter's Bitters	6c Schroeder's Bitters	6d Kintzing Bitters	6e Kintzing Bitters	6f Udolpho-wolfe's Schnapps
Shape and distinctive markings							
Base:							
Vertical cross-section	ac	ace	ace	ace	ace	ace	ae
Horizontal cross-section ..	j	j	j	j	j	j	j
Markings	s	s	st	t	s	t	t
Body:							
Vertical cross-section							
Horizontal cross-section ..	nv	nv	nv	n	n	nv	n
Markings	zaa	zaa		zaadd	zaa	zaa	zaa
Shoulder:							
Vertical cross-section	f	f	f	f	f	f	f
Horizontal cross-section ..	k	k	k	k	k	k	g
Markings	x	x	x	x	x	x	x
Neck:							
Vertical cross-section	b	b	b	a	a	b	b
Horizontal cross-section ..	g	g	g	g	g	g	g
Markings	v	v	1	v	1	v	1
Neck finish (see fig. 2)	1	1	1	1	1	1	1
Material	2ae	2ae	2ae	2ae	2ae	2ae	2ae
Color	1,7	7	1,7	7	7	1	7
Dimensions (in inches)							
Height:							
Base to shoulder	6-1/4	7-1/8	6-3/4	7-1/16	6-3/16	6-3/4	5-15/16
Shoulder to neck terminus	2-5/8	2-3/16	3	2-7/8	2-11/16	3	2-1/8
Width of sides	2-5/8	2-13/16	2-7/8	3-1/16	2-13/16	2-7/8	2-3/8
Diameter of neck:							
Outside	1-1/8	1-1/16	1-1/16	1	1	1	1
Inside	3/4	3/4	sealed	3/4	11/16	3/4	3/4
Capacity to brim (in ounces) .	22	28	28-1/2	32-1/2	26	26	15
Label	paper/relief	paper/relief	none	paper	relief	none	relief
Stopper	c	cjl	cjl	cm	c	c	c
Case marks	yes	none	yes	yes	yes	yes	yes

Distinctive features: Type 6, French square; Subtype 6d, "C.S. Kintzing/St. Louis Mo." on body.

TABLE 7—Class III (Types 7, 8 and 9) bottle features.

	Type and Subtypes			
	7	8	9	9a
General description	Drake's Bitters	Kelly's Bitters	Schroeder's Bitters	Schroeder's Bitters
Shape and distinctive markings				
Base:				
Vertical cross-section	ac	ac	c	c
Horizontal cross-section	ij	i	f	f
Markings	t	t	t	
Body:				
Vertical cross-section	i	i	ae	ae
Horizontal cross-section	nv	mv	j	j
Markings	zaacc	zcc	zaa	
Shoulder:				
Vertical cross-section	c		f	f
Horizontal cross-section	k	j	g	g
Markings	wy	wxy	x	x
Neck:				
Vertical cross-section	a	a	c	c
Horizontal cross-section	g	g	g	g
Markings			v	v
Neck finish (see fig. 2)	1	1	13	13
Material.............................	2a	2ae	2ae	2a
Color................................	1	1	1	1
Dimensions (in inches)				
Height:				
Base to shoulder	6	5-1/4	5-1/16	5-1/4
Shoulder to neck terminus	3-7/8	3-7/8	6-7/8	6-1/2
Diam. of base or width of sides	2-3/4x2-3/4	2-3/4x3-7/16	3-3/8	3-1/2
Diameter of neck:				
Outside	1-1/16	1	1-1/16	1-1/8
Inside	13/16	3/4	3/4	3/4
Capacity to brim (in ounces)..............	27	25	28	29
Label................................	paper/relief	paper	paper/relief	none
Stopper	c	c	cm	cm
Case marks	yes	yes	yes	yes

Distinctive features: Type 7, formed as a log cabin; Type 8, formed as a log cabin; Type 9, "Schroeder's Spice Bitters" in relief.

TABLE 8—Class IV (Type 1) bottle features.

General description	Types and Subtypes		
	1	1a	1b
General description	perfume vials	perfume vials	perfume vials
Shape and distinctive markings			
Base:			
Vertical cross-section	a	a	a
Horizontal cross-section	f	f	f
Markings	u	u	u
Body:			
Vertical cross-section	a	a	a
Horizontal cross-section	j	j	j
Markings			
Shoulder:			
Vertical cross-section	d	d	d
Horizontal cross-section	g	g	g
Markings			
Neck:			
Vertical cross-section	a	a	a
Horizontal cross-section	g	g	g
Markings			
Neck finish (see fig. 2)	24	24	24
Material	2a	2a	2a
Color	6	6	6
Dimensions (in inches)			
Height:			
Base to shoulder	1-1/8	2-1/16	1-1/8
Shoulder to neck terminus	1/4	5/16	1/4
Diameter of base	3/8	5/8	5/16
Diameter of neck:			
Outside	7/16	5/8	3/8
Inside	1/4	3/8	1/4
Capacity to brim (in ounces)	.1	.3	.07
Label	none	none	none
Stopper	c	c	c
Case marks	yes	yes	yes

Distinctive features: none

TABLE 9—Class V (Types 1-8) bottle features.

				Type and Subtypes				
	1	2	3	4	5	6	7	8
General description	brandied peaches	brandied peaches and cherries	brandied cherries	catsup	catsup	catsup	mustard	pickles
Shape and distinctive markings								
Base:								
Vertical cross-section	c	c	c	c	c	c	c	ace
Horizontal cross-section	f	f	f	f	f	f	f	j
Markings				t	t	t		
Body:								
Vertical cross-section	a	a	ae	ae	e	a	bi	nv
Horizontal cross-section	j	j	j	t	jtw	j	j	zaacc
Markings			aa	aa	aa	aa	aa	
Shoulder:								
Vertical cross-section	b	f	b	b	b	f	a	be
Horizontal cross-section	g	g	g	g	g	g		k
Markings		x	x	x	t	x		
Neck:								
Vertical cross-section	b	a	a	a	a	a	f	a
Horizontal cross-section	g	g	g	g	g	g		g
Markings		v						
Neck finish (see fig. 2)	16	4	21	1	13	1	36	25
Material	2a	2ae	2ae	2ae	2ae	2ae	2a	2ae
Color	3,6	3	3	3	3	3	6	3
Dimensions (in inches)								
Height:								
Base to shoulder	4-3/4	6-3/8	6-1/2	5-1/2	6-9/16	4-1/2	3-1/4	5-1/4
Shoulder to neck terminus	6-1/8	4-9/16	4-3/4	6-7/16	5-11/16	4	1-1/4	6
Diam. of base or width of sides	3-1/4	2-15/16	3	2-9/16	est. 2-1/2	2-3/8	2-1/4	3-3/16 x 3-3/16
Diameter of neck:								
Outside	2-7/8	1-7/16	1-9/16	15/16	1-1/16	7/8	1-3/4	2-1/8
Inside	2-3/8	1-1/8	1-1/4	11/16	11/16	5/8	1-9/16	1-13/16
Capacity to brim (in ounces)	est. 32 sealed	25	est. 25	23	21-2/3	9-1/2	9	41
Label	paper	none	none	paper once	paper once	paper	yes	paper
Stopper	ck	c	cj	c	c	c	ck	ck
Case marks	yes	none	yes	yes	yes	yes	yes	none

Distinctive features: Type 1, kick-up base; Type 7, barrel-shaped; Type 8, plain with vine motif frame.

TABLE 10—Class V (Type 9) bottle features.

				Type and Subtypes				
	9	9a	9b	9c	9d	9e	9f	9g
General description	pickles	pickles	pickles or vegetables	pickles	pickles	honey	honey	pickles or honey
Shape and distinctive markings								
Base:								
Vertical cross-section	ace	ace	ace	ac	ace	ace	ace	ace
Horizontal cross-section	j	j	j	j	j	j	j	j
Markings	st	t	t	t	t	t	t	t
Body:								
Vertical cross-section	nv	nv	nv	nv	nv	nv	nv	nv
Horizontal cross-section	zaacc	zaacc	zaacc	zaacc	zaacc	zaacc	zaacc	zaacc
Markings								
Shoulder:								
Vertical cross-section	be	e	e	e	e	e	e	e
Horizontal cross-section	k	k	k	k	k	k	ks	k
Markings		xy	xy	xy	xy	xy	xy	xy
Neck:								
Vertical cross-section	a	a	a	a	a	a	a	a
Horizontal cross-section	g	g	g	g	g	g	g	g
Markings				v				
Neck finish (see fig. 2)	25	25	25	25	25	25	25	25
Material	2ae	2a	2a	2ae	2ae	2a	2ae	2ae
Color	3	3	3	3	3	3	3	3
Dimensions (in inches)								
Height:								
Base to shoulder	5	5-1/8	5-1/8	4-1/8	4-3/8	4	3-1/2	4-1/8
Shoulder to neck terminus	4-5/16	4	3-7/16	3-1/16	3-1/8	3-5/16	3-9/16	3-1/16
Width of sides	2-15/16	2-15/16	2-5/8	2-1/2	2-3/8	2-1/4	2-1/4	2-1/4
Diameter of neck:								
Outside	1-3/4	1-15/16	1-15/16	1-1/2	1-11/16	1-5/16	1-5/8	1-7/16
Inside	1-3/8	1-5/8	1-3/8	1-1/8	1-3/8	1-1/16	1-3/16	1-1/8
Capacity to brim (in ounces)	20	20	16	14	14	10	10	10
Label	paper	paper	paper	paper	paper	paper	paper	paper
Stopper	c	cek	cej	cek	cek	cek	cek	cek
Case marks	yes	yes	yes	yes	yes	yes	yes	yes

Distinctive features: Type 9, scalloped frame, base has backward C and R; Subtype 9a, floral motif frame; Subtype 9b, scalloped motif fleur-de-lis within; Subtype 9c, floral motif frame with no bars at end; Subtype 9d, scalloped frame; Subtype 9e, three bars on columns; Subtype 9f, latticed window motif.

TABLE 11—Class V (Types 10-14) bottle features.

	Type and Subtypes					
	10	10a	11	12	13	14
General description	Spice Mills sauce	Spice Mills sauce	pepper sauce	Worchester sauce	London Club sauce	lemon syrup
Shape and distinctive markings						
Base:						
Vertical cross-section	ace	ace	c	ce	ce	c
Horizontal cross-section	j	j	l	f	f	f
Markings	t	t	t	t	t	s
Body:						
Vertical cross-section				a	a	a
Horizontal cross-section	nv	nv	pv		j	j
Markings	zaacc	zaacc	zcc	zaa	zaa	aa
Shoulder:						
Vertical cross-section	e	e	e	f	f	f
Horizontal cross-section	ks	ks	ms	g	g	g
Markings	wy	wy	wy	x	x	x
Neck:						
Vertical cross-section	a	a	a	a	b	b
Horizontal cross-section	g	g	g	g	g	g
Markings				v		
Neck finish (see fig. 2)	28	28	28	30	28	1
Material	2ae	2ae	2ae	2ae	2a	2ae
Color	7	3,7	3	3	3	3
Dimensions (in inches)						
Height:						
Base to shoulder	2-7/8	3	3-1/8	4-1/2	3-7/8	5-9/16
Shoulder to neck terminus	5-3/4	5-5/8	5-5/8	4	3-1/4	4-11/16
Diam. of base or width of sides ..	1-7/8x1-7/8	1-1/8x1-1/8	1-3/16	2-9/16	2	2-9/16
Diameter of neck:						
Outside	1-1/8	1-1/16	1-3/16	1	1-3/8	15/16
Inside	11/16	3/4	3/4	5/8	9/16	3/4
Capacity to brim (in ounces)	5	4	6-1/2	12-1/3	6-1/2	16
Label	yes	yes	none	yes	yes	none
Stopper	c	c	c	b	c	c
Case marks	yes	yes	yes	none	yes	yes

Distinctive features: Type 10, "Western/Spice/Mills" on body; Subtype 10a, "St. Louis/Spice/Mills" on body; Type 12, "Lea & Perrins" on stopper, "E. F. Dixie" on bottle.

TABLE 12—Class V (Types 15-19) bottle features.

	15	16	17	18	19
			Type and Subtypes		
General description	black pepper	horseradish	olive oil	lemon oil	jelly
Shape and distinctive markings					
Base:					
Vertical cross-section	a	a	c	a	c
Horizontal cross-section	q	f	f	f	f
Markings	t	t			tu
Body:					
Vertical cross-section		a	ae	a	a
Horizontal cross-section	uw	j	j	j	j
Markings		zaa		aa	aa
Shoulder:					
Vertical cross-section	b	b	f	b	f
Horizontal cross-section	r	g	g	g	g
Markings		x		x	x
Neck:					
Vertical cross-section	a	a	b	a	b
Horizontal cross-section	g	g	g	g	g
Markings		v			x
Neck finish (see fig. 2)	26	20	26	26	26
Material	2ae	2ae	2ae	2ae	2ae
Color	3	3	7	3,6	3
Dimensions (in inches)					
Height:					
Base to shoulder	4	3-5/8	5-7/8	1-1/8	3-1/8
Shoulder to neck terminus ...	2-3/4	1-1/4	3-3/8	1	1-7/8
Diam. of base or width of sides	1-5/8 x 5/8 x 15/16	2-1/8	1-15/16	7/8	1-13/16
Diameter of neck:					
Outside	1-1/4	1-5/16	7/8	5/8	1-1/2
Inside	1	1-1/8	5/8	3/8	1-1/4
Capacity to brim (in ounces) ...	8-2/3	7	8-2/3	1/2	5-2/3
Label	paper	none	none	none	paper
Stopper	cm	cc	ci	c	c
Case marks	yes	yes	yes	none	yes

Distinctive features: Type 16, irregular mark on base; Type 17, kick-up in base.

TABLE 13—Classes VI and VII bottle features.

	Class VI		Class VII		
Type and Subtypes	1	2	1	2	3
General description	ink-glass	ink-ceramic	chemical bottles	essence of ginger	prescription bottles
Shape and distinctive markings					
Base:					
Vertical cross-section	a	a	c	a	a
Horizontal cross-section	m	f	f	g	i
Markings	t		t	t	t
Body:					
Vertical cross-section		a	a	b	
Horizontal cross-section	q	j	j		mv
Markings		y		aa	zaa
Shoulder:					
Vertical cross-section	f	b	f	f	f
Horizontal cross-section	n	g	g	h	j
Markings	x			x	x
Neck:					
Vertical cross-section	a	b	a	a	a
Horizontal cross-section	g	g	g	g	g
Markings	v				
Neck finish (see fig. 2)	9	22	9	9	9
Material	2a	1a	2ae	2ae	2ae
Color	3	4	3	3	6
Dimensions (in inches)					
Height:					
Base to shoulder	1-1/4	4-15/16	6-1/4	3-1/4	2-13/16
Shoulder to neck terminus ...	1-1/8	2-1/16	3	2	1-1/8
Diam. of base or width of sides	1-13/16	3	3-3/4	2-1/8x1-3/8	1-9/16x15/16
Diameter of neck:					
Outside	7/8	1-13/16	1-1/2	1-1/16	15/16
Inside	1/2	1	15/16	7/16	3/8
Capacity to brim (in ounces) ...	2	14	38	4	1-3/4
Label	none	relief/paper	none	paper	relief
Stopper	c	cm	a	c	c
Case marks	yes	yes	yes	yes	yes

Distinctive features: Class VI, Type 2, cork covered by clay substance; Class VII, Type 3, lettered "Burnett" on one side, "Boston" on other.

U.S. GOVERNMENT PRINTING OFFICE : 1975 O - 571-225